F. SCOTT FITZGERALD

CORNELSEN
SENIOR
ENGLISH
LIBRARY

The Great
Gatsby

AF178504

Cornelsen

F. Scott Fitzgerald **The Great Gatsby**

Herausgegeben von:
Hans Gerber

Verlagsredaktion:
Neil Porter

Technische Umsetzung:
Ingo Ostermaier

Umschlagkonzept:
Cornelsen Verlag GmbH

Umschlaggestaltung:
Klein & Halm Grafikdesign

Umschlagfoto:
Shutterstock.com/Maram

Herausgeber der Cornelsen Senior English Library:
Prof. Dr. Albert-Reiner Glaap

Die Originalausgabe ist 1925 im Verlag Charles Scribner's Sons erschienen.

www.cornelsen.de

2. Auflage, 11. Druck 2026

Alle Drucke dieser Auflage sind inhaltlich unverändert
und können im Unterricht nebeneinander verwendet werden.

Druck: H. Heenemann, Berlin

ISBN 978-3-06-031203-0

Contents

Then wear the gold hat, if that will move her;
     If you can bounce high, bounce for her too,
Till she cry "Lover, gold-hatted, high-bouncing lover,
     I must have you!"

THOMAS PARKE D'INVILLIERS

ONCE AGAIN
TO
ZELDA

Abbreviations and Annotations

adj	adjective	**infml**	informal
adv	adverb	**jdm/jdn**	jemandem/en
AE	American English	**n**	noun
cf.	confer; see	**p., pp.**	page, pages
derog	derogatory	**pl**	plural
e.g.	exempli gratia; for example	**sb.**	somebody
esp.	especially	**sl**	slang
etc.	et cetera; and so on	**sth.**	something
fml	formal	**usu.**	usually
i.e.	id est; in other words	**v**	verb

The annotations are arranged chronologically; the first time a word is used is where you will find it explained. All pronunciations given are American English.

Chapter 1

In my younger and more vulnerable years my father gave me some advice that I've been turning over in my mind ever since.

"Whenever you feel like criticizing anyone," he told me, "just remember that all the people in this world haven't had the advantages that you've had."

He didn't say any more but we've always been unusually communicative in a reserved way and I understood that he meant a great deal more than that. In consequence I'm inclined to reserve all judgements, a habit that has opened up many curious natures to me and also made me the victim of not a few veteran bores. The abnormal mind is quick to detect and attach itself to this quality when it appears in a normal person, and so it came about that in college I was unjustly accused of being a politician, because I was privy to the secret griefs of wild, unknown men. Most of the confidences were unsought—frequently I have feigned sleep, preoccupation or a hostile levity when I realized by some unmistakable sign that an intimate revelation was quivering on the horizon—for the intimate revelations of young men or at least the terms in which they express them are usually plagiaristic and marred by obvious suppressions. Reserving judgements is a matter of infinite hope. I am still a little afraid of missing something if I forget that, as my father snobbishly suggested and I snobbishly repeat, a sense of the fundamental decencies is parcelled out unequally at birth.

Thomas Parke D'Invilliers: the epigraph poem was written by F. Scott Fitzgerald. D'Invilliers is a character in *This Side of Paradise*, Scott Fitzgerald's first novel (1920) 1 **vulnerable**: easily hurt or wounded   8 **be inclined to**: be likely to   10 **veteran bore**: (here) sb. who is always uninteresting   13 **be privy to sth.** ['prɪvi]: share in the secret of sth.   14 **unsought** (fml): not looked for   15 **feign sth.**: pretend (to have or do) sth.   **levity** (fml): lack of seriousness   16 **revelation**: act of making sth. known   **quiver**: vibrate   18 **plagiaristic** ['pleɪdʒərɪstik]: copied from other people   **marred** (adj): damaged   22 **parcel sth. out**: divide sth. into portions

And, after boasting this way of my tolerance, I come to the admission that it has a limit. Conduct may be founded on the hard rock or the wet marshes but after a certain point I don't care what it's founded on. When I came back from the East last autumn I felt that I wanted the world to be in uniform and at a sort of moral attention forever; I wanted no more 5
riotous excursions with privileged glimpses into the human heart. Only Gatsby, the man who gives his name to this book, was exempt from my reaction—Gatsby who represented everything for which I have an unaffected scorn. If personality is an unbroken series of successful gestures, then there was something gorgeous about him, some heightened 10
sensitivity to the promises of life, as if he were related to one of those intricate machines that register earthquakes ten thousand miles away. This responsiveness had nothing to do with that flabby impressionability which is dignified under the name of the "creative temperament"—it was an extraordinary gift for hope, a romantic readiness such as I have 15
never found in any other person and which it is not likely I shall ever find again. No—Gatsby turned out all right at the end; it is what preyed on Gatsby, what foul dust floated in the wake of his dreams that temporarily closed out my interest in the abortive sorrows and short-winded elations of men. 20

My family have been prominent, well-to-do people in this middle-western city for three generations. The Carraways are something of a clan and we have a tradition that we're descended from the Dukes of Buccleuch, but the actual founder of my line was my grandfather's brother who came here in fifty-one, sent a substitute to the Civil War 25
and started the wholesale hardware business that my father carries on today.

I never saw this great-uncle but I'm supposed to look like him—with special reference to the rather hard-boiled painting that hangs in Father's office. I graduated from New Haven in 1915, just a quarter of a century 30
after my father, and a little later I participated in that delayed Teutonic migration known as the Great War. I enjoyed the counter-raid so thoroughly that I came back restless. Instead of being the warm center of the world the middle-west now seemed like the ragged edge of the universe—so I decided to go east and learn the bond business. Everybody 35
I knew was in the bond business so I supposed it could support one

more single man. All my aunts and uncles talked it over as if they were choosing a prep-school for me and finally said "Why—ye-es" with very grave, hesitant faces. Father agreed to finance me for a year and after
40   various delays I came east, permanently, I thought, in the spring of twenty-two.

The practical thing was to find rooms in the city but it was a warm season and I had just left a country of wide lawns and friendly trees, so when a young man at the office suggested that we take a house together
45   in a commuting town it sounded like a great idea. He found the house, a weather-beaten cardboard bungalow at eighty a month, but at the last minute the firm ordered him to Washington and I went out to the country alone. I had a dog, at least I had him for a few days until he ran away, and an old Dodge and a Finnish woman who made my bed and
50   cooked breakfast and muttered Finnish wisdom to herself over the electric stove.

It was lonely for a day or so until one morning some man, more recently arrived than I, stopped me on the road.

"How do you get to West Egg Village?" he asked helplessly.

55   I told him. And as I walked on I was lonely no longer. I was a guide, a pathfinder, an original settler. He had casually conferred on me the freedom of the neighborhood.

And so with the sunshine and the great bursts of leaves growing on the trees—just as things grow in fast movies—I had that familiar
60   conviction that life was beginning over again with the summer.

---

2 **conduct** ['--] (n): (moral) behaviour   3 **marsh**: Sumpf   6 **riotous**: disorderly
7 **exempt from sth.**: not bound by sth.   9 **scorn**: strong contempt   10 **gorgeous**
(infml): wonderful   12 **intricate**: difficult to understand; complicated
13 **responsiveness**: ability to react readily to sth.   **flabby** (derog): feeble and
weak   17–18 **prey on sb./sth.**: (here) to have a destructive influence on sb./sth.
18 **foul dust**: rotten, ugly worthlessness   19 **abortive**: fruitless; coming to nothing
29 **hard-boiled** (infml): not effected by sentiment   30 **New Haven**: Yale University
in New Haven, Connecticut. In the 1920s Yalemen referred to their university in this
way.   31 **Teutonic** [tuˈtɑːnɪk]: German(ic)   32 **counter-raid**: sudden surprise attack
in the opposite direction   34 **ragged**: having an uneven outline   35 **bond
business**: *Aktiengeschäft*   45 **commuting town**: town from which one travels to
one's work   46 **cardboard**: (here) not strong or solid   49 **Dodge**: well-built car for
middleclass buyers   56 **confer sth. on sb.**: give or grant sth. to sb.

There was so much to read for one thing and so much fine health to be pulled down out of the young breath-giving air. I bought a dozen volumes on banking and credit and investment securities and they stood on my shelf in red and gold like new money from the mint, promising to unfold the shining secrets that only Midas and Morgan and Mæcenas ⁵ knew. And I had the high intention of reading many other books besides. I was rather literary in college—one year I wrote a series of very solemn and obvious editorials for the "Yale News"—and now I was going to bring back all such things into my life and become again that most limited of all specialists, the "well-rounded" man. This isn't just an ¹⁰ epigram—life is much more successfully looked at from a single window, after all.

It was a matter of chance that I should have rented a house in one of the strangest communities in North America. It was on that slender riotous island which extends itself due east of New York and where ¹⁵ there are, among other natural curiosities, two unusual formations of land. Twenty miles from the city a pair of enormous eggs, identical in contour and separated only by a courtesy bay, jut out into the most domesticated body of salt water in the Western Hemisphere, the great wet barnyard of Long Island Sound. They are not perfect ovals—like the ²⁰ egg in the Columbus story they are both crushed flat at the contact end—but their physical resemblance must be a source of perpetual confusion to the gulls that fly overhead. To the wingless a more arresting phenomenon is their dissimilarity in every particular except shape and size. ²⁵

I lived at West Egg, the—well, the less fashionable of the two, though this is a most superficial tag to express the bizarre and not a little sinister contrast between them. My house was at the very tip of the egg, only fifty yards from the Sound, and squeezed between two huge places that rented for twelve or fifteen thousand a season. The one on my right was ³⁰ a colossal affair by any standard—it was a factual imitation of some Hôtel de Ville in Normandy, with a tower on one side, spanking new under a thin beard of raw ivy, and a marble swimming pool and more than forty acres of lawn and garden. It was Gatsby's mansion. Or rather, as I didn't know Mr. Gatsby, it was a mansion inhabited by a gentleman ³⁵ of that name. My own house was an eye-sore, but it was a small eye-sore and it had been overlooked, so I had a view of the water, a partial view of my neighbor's lawn and the consoling proximity of millionaires—all for eighty dollars a month.

40   Across the courtesy bay the white palaces of fashionable East Egg glittered along the water and the history of the summer really begins on the evening I drove over there to have dinner with the Tom Buchanans. Daisy was my second cousin once removed and I'd known Tom in college. And just after the war I spent two days with them in Chicago.

45   Her husband, among various physical accomplishments, had been one of the most powerful ends that ever played football at New Haven— a national figure in a way, one of those men who reach such an acute limited excellence at twenty-one that everything afterwards savours of anti-climax. His family were enormously wealthy—even in college his
50   freedom with money was a matter for reproach—but now he'd left Chicago and come east in a fashion that rather took your breath away: for instance he'd brought down a string of polo ponies from Lake Forest.

1 **for one thing**: (here) be a reason for sth.   5 **Midas**: mythical king whose touch turned everything into gold   **Morgan = J. P. Morgan** (1837–1913): American financier   **Mæcenas = Gaius Cilnius Mæcenas** (70?–8 B.C.): Roman statesman and patron of writers, e.g. Horace and Virgil   7 **literary**: familiar with literature   8 **"Yale News"**: Yale university newspaper   10 **well-rounded**: showing interest or ability in many fields   11 **epigram**: short poem or statement saying sth. in a clever and amusing way   14–15 **slender riotous island**: Long Island, which was well-known for the parties of its rich inhabitants   18 **contour**: shape   **courtesy bay**: (here) bay which is peaceful   **jut out**: stick out   19 **domesticated**: (here) tame, peaceful   20 **barnyard**: usually fenced-in area around a barn   21 **Columbus story**: Christopher Columbus supposedly responded to the remark that other men could have made his voyage by challenging the company to stand an egg on its end. When they failed, Columbus succeeded by flattening one end of the egg. The point of this demonstration was that after he had shown the way, the others could follow.   **crush sth.**: squeeze or press sth. with force   21–22 **contact end**: thicker end (of an egg)   23 **gull = seagull   arresting** (adj): attracting attention; striking   27 **tag**: (here) phrase   **sinister**: suggesting evil   31 **factual**: based on facts, actual   32 **Hôtel de Ville**: city hall or municipal building in France   **spanking** (adv) (infml): totally   36 **eye-sore**: sth. that is unpleasant to look at   37 **overlook sth.**: fail to notice sth.   38 **console sb.**: give comfort to sb.   **proximity**: closeness   43 **second cousin once removed**: second cousin's child   45 **accomplishment**: sth. one has achieved   46 **end**: (in American football) player at either end of the line   48 **savour of sth.**: have a (esp. bad) trace of sth.   50 **reproach**: expression of disapproval   52 **a string of sth.** (esp. horses): a number of sth.   **Lake Forest**: fashionable suburb of Chicago

It was hard to realize that a man in my own generation was wealthy enough to do that.

Why they came east I don't know. They had spent a year in France, for no particular reason, and then drifted here and there unrestfully wherever people played polo and were rich together. This was a perman- ⁵ ent move, said Daisy over the telephone, but I didn't believe it—I had no sight into Daisy's heart but I felt that Tom would drift on forever seeking a little wistfully for the dramatic turbulence of some irrecoverable football game.

And so it happened that on a warm windy evening I drove over to ¹⁰ East Egg to see two old friends whom I scarcely knew at all. Their house was even more elaborate than I expected, a cheerful red and white Georgian Colonial mansion overlooking the bay. The lawn started at the beach and ran toward the front door for a quarter of a mile, jumping over sun-dials and brick walks and burning gardens—finally when it ¹⁵ reached the house drifting up the side in bright vines as though from the momentum of its run. The front was broken by a line of French windows, glowing now with reflected gold, and wide open to the warm windy afternoon, and Tom Buchanan in riding clothes was standing with his legs apart on the front porch. ²⁰

He had changed since his New Haven years. Now he was a sturdy, straw-haired man of thirty with a rather hard mouth and a supercilious manner. Two shining, arrogant eyes had established dominance over his face and gave him the appearance of always leaning aggressively forward. Not even the effeminate swank of his riding clothes could hide the ²⁵ enormous power of that body—he seemed to fill those glistening boots until he strained the top lacing and you could see a great pack of muscle shifting when his shoulder moved under his thin coat. It was a body capable of enormous leverage—a cruel body.

His speaking voice, a gruff husky tenor, added to the impression of ³⁰ fractiousness he conveyed. There was a touch of paternal contempt in it, even toward people he liked—and there were men at New Haven who had hated his guts.

"Now, don't think my opinion on these matters is final," he seemed to say, "just because I'm stronger and more of a man than you are." We ³⁵ were in the same Senior Society and while we were never intimate I always had the impression that he approved of me and wanted me to like him with some harsh, defiant wistfulness of his own.

We talked for a few minutes on the sunny porch.

40 "I've got a nice place here," he said, his eyes flashing about restlessly.

Turning me around by one arm he moved a broad flat hand along the front vista, including in its sweep a sunken Italian garden, a half acre of deep pungent roses and a snub-nosed motor boat that bumped the tide off shore.

45 "It belonged to Demaine the oil man." He turned me around again, politely and abruptly. "We'll go inside."

We walked through a high hallway into a bright rosy-colored space, fragilely bound into the house by French windows at either end. The windows were ajar and gleaming white against the fresh grass outside

50 that seemed to grow a little way into the house. A breeze blew through the room, blew curtains in at one end and out the other like pale flags, twisting them up toward the frosted wedding cake of the ceiling—and then rippled over the wine-colored rug, making a shadow on it as wind does on the sea.

55 The only completely stationary object in the room was an enormous couch on which two young women were buoyed up as though upon an

---

8 **wistfully**: full of vague longing   12 **elaborate**: (here) highly ornamented
16 **vine**: climbing plant   17 **momentum of its run**: power or strength of the
direction of sth.   17–18 **French window**: door with long glass panes, usu. opening
onto a garden or a balcony   21 **sturdy**: strong   22 **supercilious** [ˌsuːpərˈsɪliəs]:
arrogant and disdainful   25 **effeminate**: unmanly; like a woman   **swank**: (here)
stylish, showy   27 **strain sth.**: stretch sth. tightly by pulling   **top lacing**: tied cord
or lace on a shoe, etc.   29 **leverage** [ˈlevərɪdʒ]: power; influence   30 **gruff**: rough
husky: sounding lightly hoarse; dry in the throat   31 **fractiousness**: being hard to
manage; rebellious   **paternal**: fatherly; of a father   **contempt**: feeling that sb./sth.
cannot be respected   33 **hate sb.'s guts** (infml): dislike sb. intensely   36 **Senior
Society**: there were six senior societies at Yale; each elected 15 men at the end of
their junior year. Election to a senior society was the highest social achievement at
Yale.   38 **defiant**: openly challenging   42 **vista** (fml): view   **sweep** (n): movement
over an area   43 **pungent**: strong smelling   **snub-nosed**: short and turned up
slightly at the end   **bump the tide**: (here move up and down on the waves
48 **fragile**: delicate   49 **ajar**: slightly open   52 **frosted wedding cake of the
ceiling**: a ceiling that looks like a decorated wedding cake   53 **ripple**: move in
ripples, i.e. in series of waves   **rug**: thick small carpet   56 **buoyed up**: supported
(buoy = *Boje*)

anchored balloon. They were both in white and their dresses were rippling and fluttering as if they had just been blown back in after a short flight around the house. I must have stood for a few moments listening to the whip and snap of the curtains and the groan of a picture on the wall. Then there was a boom as Tom Buchanan shut the rear win- 5 dows and the caught wind died out about the room and the curtains and the rugs and the two young women ballooned slowly to the floor.

The younger of the two was a stranger to me. She was extended full length at her end of the divan, completely motionless and with her chin raised a little as if she were balancing something on it which was quite 10 likely to fall. If she saw me out of the corner of her eyes she gave no hint of it—indeed I was almost surprised into murmuring an apology for having disturbed her by coming in.

The other girl, Daisy, made an attempt to rise—she leaned slightly forward with a conscientious expression—then she laughed, an absurd, 15 charming little laugh, and I laughed too and came forward into the room.

"I'm p-paralyzed with happiness."

She laughed again, as if she said something very witty, and held my hand for a moment, looking up into my face, promising that there was 20 no one in the world she so much wanted to see. That was a way she had. She hinted in a murmur that the surname of the balancing girl was Baker. (I've heard it said that Daisy's murmur was only to make people lean toward her; an irrelevant criticism that made it no less charming.)

At any rate Miss Baker's lips fluttered, she nodded at me almost 25 imperceptibly and then quickly tipped her head back again—the object she was balancing had obviously tottered a little and given her something of a fright. Again a sort of apology arose to my lips. Almost any exhibition of complete self-sufficiency draws a stunned tribute from me.

I looked back at my cousin who began to ask me questions in her 30 low, thrilling voice. It was the kind of voice that the ear follows up and down as if each speech is an arrangement of notes that will never be played again. Her face was sad and lovely with bright things in it, bright eyes and a bright passionate mouth—but there was an excitement in her voice that men who had cared for her found difficult to forget: a 35 singing compulsion, a whispered "Listen," a promise that she had done gay, exciting things just a while since and that there were gay, exciting things hovering in the next hour.

I told her how I had stopped off in Chicago for a day on my way east
40 and how a dozen people had sent their love through me.

"Do they miss me?" she cried ecstatically.

"The whole town is desolate. All the cars have the left rear wheel painted black as a mourning wreath and there's a persistent wail all night along the North Shore."

45 "How gorgeous! Let's go back, Tom. Tomorrow!" Then she added irrelevantly, "You ought to see the baby."

"I'd like to."

"She's asleep. She's two years old. Haven't you ever seen her?"

"Never."

50 "Well, you ought to see her. She's——"

Tom Buchanan who had been hovering restlessly about the room stopped and rested his hand on my shoulder.

"What you doing, Nick?"

"I'm a bond man."

55 "Who with?"

I told him.

"Never heard of them," he remarked decisively.

This annoyed me.

"You will," I answered shortly. "You will if you stay in the East."

60 "Oh, I'll stay in the East, don't you worry," he said, glancing at Daisy and then back at me as if he were alert for something more. "I'd be a God Damn fool to live anywhere else."

---

4 **whip and snap**: sudden movements resulting in sharp noises   **groan**: deep sound
15 **conscientious** [ˌkɑːnʃiˈenʃəs]: showing care and precision   25 **flutter**: move lightly and quickly   26 **imperceptible**: that cannot be noticed because it is small or slight   27 **totter**: move unsteadily   28 **fright**: feeling of sudden fear   29 **self sufficiency**: ability to fulfil one's needs, without help from others   **draw sth. from sb.**: produce sth. (esp. a reaction) from sb.   **stunned**: shocked by sth. unexpected
36 **compulsion**: urge one cannot resist   38 **hover**: (here) wait   43 **mourning wreath**: *Trauerkranz*   **wail** (n): sad crying sound   44 **North Shore**: fashionable area of Chicago along the northern shore of Lake Michigan   51 **hover about**: move around   61 **alert**: watchful and prepared

At this point Miss Baker said "Absolutely!" with such suddenness
that I started—it was the first word she had uttered since I came into the
room. Evidently it surprised her as much as it did me, for she yawned
and with a series of rapid, deft movements stood up into the room.

"I'm stiff," she complained. "I've been lying on that sofa for as long as 5
I can remember."

"Don't look at me," Daisy retorted. "I've been trying to get you to New
York all afternoon."

"No thanks," said Miss Baker to the four cocktails just in from the
pantry, "I'm absolutely in training." 10

Her host looked at her incredulously.

"You are!" He took down his drink as if it were a drop in the bottom
of a glass. "How you ever get anything done is beyond me."

I looked at Miss Baker wondering what it was she "got done." I
enjoyed looking at her. She was a slender, small-breasted girl with an 15
erect carriage which she accentuated by throwing her body backward at
the shoulders like a young cadet. Her grey sun-strained eyes looked
back at me with polite reciprocal curiosity out of a wan, charming dis-
contented face. It occurred to me now that I had seen her, or a picture
of her, somewhere before. 20

"You live in West Egg," she remarked contemptuously. "I know
somebody there."

"I don't know a single——"

"You must know Gatsby."

"Gatsby?" demanded Daisy. "What Gatsby?" 25

Before I could reply that he was my neighbor dinner was announced;
wedging his tense arm imperatively under mine, Tom Buchanan compelled me from the room as though he were moving a checker to another
square.

Slenderly, languidly, their hands set lightly on their hips, the two 30
young women preceded us out onto a rosy-colored porch open toward
the sunset where four candles flickered on the table in the diminished
wind.

"Why *candles*?" objected Daisy frowning. She snapped them out with
her fingers. "In two weeks it'll be the longest day in the year." She looked 35
at us all radiantly. "Do you always watch for the longest day of the year

and then miss it? I always watch for the longest day in the year and then miss it."

"We ought to plan something," yawned Miss Baker, sitting down at the table as if she were getting into bed.

"All right," said Daisy. "What'll we plan?" She turned to me helplessly. "What do people plan?"

Before I could answer her eyes fastened with an awed expression on her little finger.

"Look!" she complained. "I hurt it."

We all looked—the knuckle was black and blue.

"You did it, Tom," she said accusingly. "I know you didn't mean to but you *did* do it. That's what I get for marrying a brute of a man, a great big hulking physical specimen of a——"

"I hate that word hulking," objected Tom crossly, "even in kidding."

"Hulking," insisted Daisy.

Sometimes she and Miss Baker talked at once, unobtrusively and with a bantering inconsequence that was never quite chatter, that was as cool as their white dresses and their impersonal eyes in the absence of all desire. They were here—and they accepted Tom and me, making only a polite pleasant effort to entertain or to be entertained. They knew that presently dinner would be over and a little later the evening too would be over and casually put away. It was sharply different from the West where an evening was hurried from phase to phase toward its close in a continually disappointed anticipation or else in sheer nervous dread of the moment itself.

---

4 **deft**: skilful; quick   7 **retort**: make a witty or angry remark   10 **pantry**: (here) room where glass, silver, table-linen, etc. are kept   11 **incredulous**: showing disbelief   16 **carriage**: (here) posture   17 **sun-strained**: eyes are screwed up because of the sun   18 **reciprocal**: mutual   **wan**: colourless   27 **wedge sth. under sth. else**: put sth. under sth. else   28 **checker**: *Stein beim Damespiel* 30 **languid**: slow-moving   36 **radiant**: shining brightly   43 **awed**: filled with fear and wonder   49 **hulking**: large and heavy   **specimen**: individual; example   50 **in kidding** (infml): as a joke   52 **unobtrusive**: not easily noticeable   53 **bantering**: good-natured teasing   58 **casual**: showing little concern   60 **anticipation**: foreknowledge, expectation

"You make me feel uncivilized, Daisy," I confessed on my second glass of corky but rather impressive claret. "Can't you talk about crops or something?"

I meant nothing in particular by this remark but it was taken up in an unexpected way. 5

"Civilization's going to pieces," broke out Tom violently. "I've gotten to be a terrible pessimist about things. Have you read 'The Rise of the Coloured Empires' by this man Goddard?"

"Why, no," I answered, rather surprised by his tone.

"Well, it's a fine book and everybody ought to read it. The idea is if we 10 don't look out the white race will be—will be utterly submerged. It's all scientific stuff; it's been proved."

"Tom's getting very profound," said Daisy with an expression of unthoughtful sadness. "He reads deep books with long words in them. What was that word we——" 15

"Well, these books are all scientific," insisted Tom, glancing at her impatiently. "This fellow has worked out the whole thing. It's up to us who are the dominant race to watch out or these other races will have control of things."

"We've got to beat them down," whispered Daisy, winking ferociously 20 toward the fervent sun.

"You ought to live in California——" began Miss Baker but Tom interrupted her by shifting heavily in his chair.

"This idea is that we're Nordics. I am and you are and you are and— —" After an infinitesimal hesitation he included Daisy with a slight nod 25 and she winked at me again, "——and we've produced all the things that go to make civilization—oh, science and art and all that. Do you see?"

There was something pathetic in his concentration as if his complacency, more acute than of old, was not enough to him any more. When, almost immediately, the telephone rang inside and the butler left 30 the porch Daisy seized upon the momentary interruption and leaned toward me.

"I'll tell you a family secret," she whispered enthusiastically. "It's about the butler's nose. Do you want to hear about the butler's nose?"

"That's why I came over tonight." 35

"Well, he wasn't always a butler; he used to be the silver polisher for some people in New York that had a silver service for two hundred

people. He had to polish it from morning till night until finally it began
to affect his nose——"

40   "Things went from bad to worse," suggested Miss Baker.

"Yes. Things went from bad to worse until finally he had to give up
his position."

For a moment the last sunshine fell with romantic affection upon her
glowing face; her voice compelled me forward breathlessly as I listened—
45   then the glow faded, each light deserting her with lingering regret like
children leaving a pleasant street at dusk.

The butler came back and murmured something close to Tom's ear
whereupon Tom frowned, pushed back his chair and without a word
went inside. As if his absence quickened something within her Daisy
50   leaned forward again, her voice glowing and singing.

"I love to see you at my table, Nick. You remind me of a—of a rose, an
absolute rose. Doesn't he?" She turned to Miss Baker for confirmation.
"An absolute rose?"

This was untrue. I am not even faintly like a rose. She was only
55   extemporizing but a stirring warmth flowed from her as if her heart was
trying to come out to you concealed in one of those breathless, thrilling
words. Then suddenly she threw her napkin on the table and excused
herself and went into the house.

Miss Baker and I exchanged a short glance consciously devoid of
60   meaning. I was about to speak when she sat up alertly and said "Sh!" in
a warning voice. A subdued impassioned murmur was audible in the
room beyond and Miss Baker leaned forward, unashamed, trying to
hear. The murmur trembled on the verge of coherence, sank down,
mounted excitedly and then ceased altogether.

2 **corky**: having the taste affected by the cork   **claret**: dry red wine from Bordeaux
7–8 **"The Rise of the Coloured Empires"**: allusion to *The Rising Tide of Colour* by
Lothrop Stoddard (1920)   11 **submerge sth.**: (here) overwhelm sth.   20 **ferocious**
[fə'rouʃəs]: fierce; violent   21 **fervent**: hot   25 **infinitesimal** [,- - - '- - -]:
extremely small   29 **complacency** [kəm'pleɪsənsi]: feeling of satisfaction with
oneself   44 **compel sb. forward**: make sb. move forward   45 **linger**: remain in
existence though becoming weaker   55 **extemporize**: speak or perform without
previous preparation   **stirring**: very exciting   56 **conceal sth.**: hide sth.
59 **devoid of**: without   61 **subdued**: not very loud   **audible**: that can be heard
63 **on the verge of**: close to sth., similar to sth.   **coherence**: state of being clear or
easy to understand

"This Mr. Gatsby you spoke of is my neighbor—" I said.

"Don't talk. I want to hear what happens."

"Is something happening?" I inquired innocently.

"You mean to say you don't know?" said Miss Baker, honestly surprised. "I thought everybody knew."   5

"I don't."

"Why—" she said hesitantly, "Tom's got some woman in New York."

"Got some woman?" I repeated blankly.

Miss Baker nodded.

"She might have the decency not to telephone him at dinner-time.   10
Don't you think?"

Almost before I had grasped her meaning there was the flutter of a dress and the crunch of leather boots and Tom and Daisy were back at the table.

"It couldn't be helped!" cried Daisy with tense gayety.   15

She sat down, glanced searchingly at Miss Baker and then at me and continued, "I looked outdoors for a minute and it's very romantic outdoors. There's a bird on the lawn that I think must be a nightingale come over on the Cunard or White Star Line. He's singing away—" her voice sang "—It's romantic, isn't it, Tom?"   20

"Very romantic," he said, and then miserably to me: "If it's light enough after dinner I want to take you down to the stables."

The telephone rang inside, startlingly, and as Daisy shook her head decisively at Tom, the subject of the stables, in fact all subjects, vanished into air. Among the broken fragments of the last five minutes at table I   25
remember the candles being lit again, pointlessly, and I was conscious of wanting to look squarely at everyone and yet to avoid all eyes. I couldn't guess what Daisy and Tom were thinking but I doubt if even Miss Baker, who seemed to have mastered a certain hardy skepticism, was able utterly to put this fifth guest's shrill metallic urgency out of mind. To a   30
certain temperament the situation might have seemed intriguing—my own instinct was to telephone immediately for the police.

The horses, needless to say, were not mentioned again. Tom and Miss Baker with several feet of twilight between them strolled back into the library, as if to a vigil beside a perfectly tangible body, while trying to   35
look pleasantly interested and a little deaf I followed Daisy around a

chain of connecting verandas to the porch in front. In its deep gloom we sat down side by side on a wicker settee.

40 Daisy took her face in her hands, as if feeling its lovely shape, and her eyes moved gradually out into the velvet dusk. I saw that turbulent emotions possessed her, so I asked what I thought would be some sedative questions about her little girl.

"We don't know each other very well, Nick," she said suddenly. "Even if we are cousins. You didn't come to my wedding."

45 "I wasn't back from the war."

"That's true." She hesitated. "Well, I've had a very bad time, Nick, and I'm pretty cynical about everything."

Evidently she had reason to be. I waited but she didn't say any more, and after a moment I returned rather feebly to the subject of her
50 daughter.

"I suppose she talks, and—eats, and everything."

"Oh, yes." She looked at me absently. "Listen, Nick; let me tell you what I said when she was born. Would you like to hear?"

"Very much."

55 "It'll show you how I've gotten to feel about—things. Well, she was less than an hour old and Tom was God knows where. I woke up out of the ether with an utterly abandoned feeling and asked the nurse right away if it was a boy or a girl. She told me it was a girl, and so I turned my head away and wept. 'All right,' I said, 'I'm glad it's a girl. And I hope
60 she'll be a fool—that's the best thing a girl can be in this world, a beautiful little fool.'

"You see I think everything's terrible anyhow," she went on in a convinced way. "Everybody thinks so—the most advanced people. And I *know*. I've been everywhere and seen everything and done everything."

---

10 **decency**: respectable behaviour   15 **gayety**: cheerfulness   18 **nightingale**: there are no nightingales in the USA   19 **Cunard** [kjuːˈnɑːrd], **White Star Line**: British-owned transatlantic shipping lines   23 **startlingly**: with a start   24 **decisive**: demonstrative, firm   26 **pointless**: with little or no sense   27 **squarely**: directly   29 **hardy**: tough, strong   30 **urgency**: state of needing immediate attention   31 **intriguing**: fascinating, interesting   35 **vigil**: period of staying awake (here) around a dead body   **tangible** (fml): that can be perceived by touch   38 **wicker settee**: long seat made of wicker (canes woven together)   41 **sedative**: having a calming effect   57 **ether**: gas used as an anaesthetic

Her eyes flashed around her in a defiant way, rather like Tom's, and she laughed with thrilling scorn. "Sophisticated—God, I'm sophisticated!"

The instant her voice broke off, ceasing to compel my attention, my belief, I felt the basic insincerity of what she had said. It made me uneasy, as though the whole evening had been a trick of some sort to exact a 5 contributary emotion from me. I waited, and sure enough, in a moment she looked at me with an absolute smirk on her lovely face as if she had asserted her membership in a rather distinguished secret society to which she and Tom belonged.

Inside, the crimson room bloomed with light. Tom and Miss Baker sat at 10 either end of the long couch and she read aloud to him from the "Saturday Evening Post"—the words, murmurous and uninflected, running together in a soothing tune. The lamp-light, bright on his boots and dull on the autumn-leaf yellow of her hair, glinted along the paper as she turned a page with a flutter of slender muscles in her arms. 15

When we came in she held us silent for a moment with a lifted hand.

"To be continued," she said, tossing the magazine on the table, "in our very next issue."

Her body asserted itself with a restless movement of her knee, and 20 she stood up.

"Ten o'clock," she remarked, apparently finding the time on the ceiling. "Time for this good girl to go to bed."

"Jordan's going to play in the tournament tomorrow," explained Daisy, "over at Westchester." 25

"Oh,—you're *Jor*dan Baker."

I knew now why her face was familiar—its pleasing contemptuous expression had looked out at me from many rotogravure pictures of the sporting life at Asheville and Hot Springs and Palm Beach. I had heard some story of her too, a critical, unpleasant story, but what it was I had 30 forgotten long ago.

"Good night," she said softly. "Wake me at eight, won't you."

"If you'll get up."

"I will. Good night, Mr. Carraway. See you anon."

"Of course you will," confirmed Daisy. "In fact I think I'll arrange a 35 marriage. Come over often, Nick, and I'll sort of—oh—fling you together. You know—lock you up accidentally in linen closets and push you out to sea in a boat, and all that sort of thing——"

"Good night," called Miss Baker from the stairs. "I haven't heard a
40 word."

"She's a nice girl," said Tom after a moment. "They oughtn't to let her run around the country this way."

"Who oughtn't to?" inquired Daisy coldly.

"Her family."

45 "Her family is one aunt about a thousand years old. Besides, Nick's going to look after her, aren't you, Nick? She's going to spend lots of week-ends out here this summer. I think the home influence will be very good for her."

Daisy and Tom looked at each other for a moment in silence.

50 "Is she from New York?" I asked quickly.

"From Louisville. Our white girlhood was passed together there. Our beautiful white——"

"Did you give Nick a little heart-to-heart talk on the veranda?" demanded Tom suddenly.

55 "Did I?" She looked at me. "I can't seem to remember, but I think we talked about the Nordic race. Yes, I'm sure we did. It sort of crept up on us and first thing you know——"

"Don't believe everything you hear, Nick," he advised me.

I said lightly that I had heard nothing at all, and a few minutes later
60 I got up to go home. They came to the door with me and stood side

---

2 **thrilling**: shivering with excitement   **sophisticated**: having a lot of worldly knowledge and experience   5 **exact sth.**: insist on and to obtain sth.
6 **contributary**: having a share in bringing about a result   7 **smirk** (n): silly or self-satisfied smile   10 **crimson**: deep red   12 **uninflected**: speaking in one tone
13 **soothing**: quieting, calming   14 **glint** (v): give out small, bright flashes of light
20 **assert oneself**: behave in a way that makes one noticed   25 **Westchester**: suburb of New York City   27 **contemptuous**: showing contempt, scorn
28 **rotogravure**: process for printing photographs in newspapers   29 **Asheville, Hot Springs, Palm Beach**: fashionable resorts in North Carolina, Arkansas and Florida   34 **anon** (old fashioned): soon   36–37 **fling sb. together**: (here) arrange that sb. come together   51 **Louisville**: city in Kentucky   56 **creep up on sb./sth.**: come gradually and almost unnoticed to sb./sth.

by side in a cheerful square of light. As I started my motor Daisy peremptorily called "Wait!

"I forgot to ask you something, and it's important. We heard you were engaged to a girl out West."

"That's right," corroborated Tom kindly. "We heard that you were 5 engaged."

"It's a libel. I'm too poor."

"But we heard it," insisted Daisy, surprising me by opening up again in a flower-like way. "We heard it from three people so it must be true."

Of course I knew what they were referring to, but I wasn't even 10 vaguely engaged. The fact that gossip had published the banns was one of the reasons I had come east. You can't stop going with an old friend on account of rumors and on the other hand I had no intention of being rumored into marriage.

Their interest rather touched me and made them less remotely rich— 15 nevertheless, I was confused and a little disgusted as I drove away. It seemed to me that the thing for Daisy to do was to rush out of the house, child in arms—but apparently there were no such intentions in her head. As for Tom the fact that he "had some woman in New York" was really less surprising than that he had been depressed by a book. 20 Something was making him nibble at the edge of stale ideas as if his sturdy physical egotism no longer nourished his peremptory heart.

Already it was deep summer on roadhouse roofs and in front of wayside garages where new red gas-pumps sat out in pools of light, and when I reached my estate at West Egg I ran the car under its shed and 25 sat for a while on an abandoned grass roller in the yard. The wind had blown off, leaving a loud bright night with wings beating in the trees and a persistent organ sound as the full bellows of the earth blew the frogs full of life. The silhouette of a moving cat wavered across the moonlight, and turning my head to watch it I saw that I was not alone— 30 fifty feet away a figure had emerged from the shadow of my neighbor's mansion and was standing with his hands in his pockets regarding the silver pepper of the stars. Something in his leisurely movements and the secure position of his feet upon the lawn suggested that it was Mr. Gatsby himself, come out to determine what share was his of our local 35 heavens.

I decided to call to him. Miss Baker had mentioned him at dinner, and that would do for an introduction. But I didn't call to him for he gave a sudden intimation that he was content to be alone—he stretched
40 out his arms toward the dark water in a curious way, and far as I was from him I could have sworn he was trembling. Involuntarily I glanced seaward—and distinguished nothing except a single green light, minute and far away, that might have been the end of a dock. When I looked once more for Gatsby he had vanished, and I was alone again in the
45 unquiet darkness.

2 **peremptory** (fml): not to be disobeyed or questioned; urgent   5 **corroborate**: support a statement, etc.   7 **libel**: false statement that damages sb.'s reputation
11 **banns** (pl.): public announcement in church that two people intend to marry each other   21 **nibble at sth.**: show some interest in sth.   **stale**: old and unfashionable   22 **egotism**: selfishness   28 **bellows** (pl.): instrument that blows air in an organ   29 **waver**: move unsteadily   39 **intimation**: hint, sign

Chapter 2

About half way between West Egg and New York, the motor-road hastily joins the railroad and runs beside it for a quarter of a mile so as to shrink away from a certain desolate area of land. This is a valley of ashes—a fantastic farm where ashes grow like wheat into ridges and hills and grotesque gardens, where ashes take the forms of houses and chimneys and rising smoke and finally, with a transcendent effort, of men who move dimly and already crumbling through the powdery air. Occasionally a line of grey cars crawls along an invisible track, gives out a ghastly creak and comes to rest, and immediately the ash-grey men swarm up with leaden spades and stir up an impenetrable cloud which screens their obscure operations from your sight.

But above the grey land and the spasms of bleak dust which drift endlessly over it, you perceive, after a moment, the eyes of Doctor T. J. Eckleburg. The eyes of Doctor T. J. Eckleburg are blue and gigantic—their retinas are one yard high. They look out of no face but, instead, from a pair of enormous yellow spectacles which pass over a nonexistent nose. Evidently some wild wag of an oculist set them there to fatten his practice in the borough of Queens and then sank down himself into eternal blindness or forgot them and moved away. But his eyes, dimmed a little by many paintless days under sun and rain, brood on over the solemn dumping ground.

The valley of ashes is bounded on one side by a small foul river, and when the drawbridge is up to let barges through, the passengers on waiting trains can stare at the dismal scene for as long as half an hour. There is always a halt there of at least a minute and it was because of this that I first met Tom Buchanan's mistress.

The fact that he had one was insisted upon wherever he was known. His acquaintances resented the fact that he turned up in popular restaurants with her and, leaving her at a table, sauntered about chatting with whomsoever he knew. Though I was curious to see her I had no desire to meet her—but I did. I went up to New York with Tom on the train one afternoon and when we stopped by the ashheaps he jumped to his feet and taking hold of my elbow literally forced me from the car.

"We're getting off!" he insisted. "I want you to meet my girl."

35   I think he'd tanked up a good deal at luncheon and his determination to have my company bordered on violence. The supercilious assumption was that on Sunday afternoon I had nothing better to do.

I followed him over a low white-washed railroad fence and we walked back a hundred yards along the road under Doctor Eckleburg's
40 persistent stare. The only building in sight was a small block of yellow brick sitting on the edge of the waste land, a sort of compact Main Street ministering to it and contiguous to absolutely nothing. One of the three shops it contained was for rent and another was an all-night restaurant approached by a trail of ashes; the third was a garage—Repairs. GEORGE
45 B. WILSON. Cars Bought and Sold—and I followed Tom inside.

The interior was unprosperous and bare; the only car visible was the dust-covered wreck of a Ford which crouched in a dim corner. It had occurred to me that this shadow of a garage must be a blind and that sumptuous and romantic apartments were concealed overhead when
50 the proprietor himself appeared in the door of an office, wiping his hands on a piece of waste. He was a blonde, spiritless man, anæmic and faintly handsome. When he saw us a damp gleam of hope sprang into his light blue eyes.

---

3 **valley of ashes**: (here) swamp which is being filled with ash   6 **transcendent** (fml): extremely great   9 **creak** (n): harsh sound (like that of an unoiled door) 10 **leaden** ['ledən]: heavy   10–11 **screen sth. from sb./sth.**: conceal, protect sth. from sb./sth.   12 **spasm**: sudden short outburst of sth.   **bleak**: dreary, gloomy, dismal   15 **retina**: *Netzhaut*   17 **wag** (old fashioned): person who is fond of making jokes   **oculist**: *Augenarzt/ärztin*   18 **Queens**: borough of New York City 20 **brood**: think (about sth.) in a troubled way   23 **barge**: Frachtkahn   24 **dismal**: miserable   26 **mistress**: (here) woman having a sexual relationship with a married man   28 **resent sth.**: feel angry about sth.   29 **saunter about**: walk in a leisurely way   33 **car** (AE): carriage   35 **tank up** (infml): become drunk   **luncheon** (fml): lunch   36 **border on sth.**: be close to sth.   42 **minister to sth.**: (here) be of service to sth.   **contiguous to sth.** [kən'tɪgjuəs] (fml): neighboring sth.   44 **trail**: path   48 **blind** (n): (here) thing used to deceive   49 **sumptuous**: expensive and splendid   51 **waste**: (here) cloth used for wiping machinery   **anaemic**: lacking strength; weak   52 **damp**: (here) *gedämpft*   **gleam**: brief appearance of some emotion

"Hello Wilson, old man," said Tom, slapping him jovially on the shoulder. "How's business?"

"I can't complain," answered Wilson unconvincingly. "When are you going to sell me that car?"

"Next week; I've got my man working on it now."   5

"Works pretty slow, don't he?"

"No, he doesn't," said Tom coldly. "And if you feel that way about it maybe I'd better sell it somewhere else after all."

"I don't mean that," explained Wilson quickly. "I just meant——"

His voice faded off and Tom glanced impatiently around the garage.   10
Then I heard footsteps on a stairs and in a moment the thickish figure of a woman blocked out the light from the office door. She was in the middle thirties, and faintly stout, but she carried her surplus flesh sensuously as some women can. Her face, above a spotted dress of dark blue crêpe-de-chine, contained no facet or gleam of beauty but there was an   15
immediately perceptible vitality about her as if the nerves of her body were continually smouldering. She smiled slowly and walking through her husband as if he were a ghost shook hands with Tom, looking him flush in the eye. Then she wet her lips and without turning around spoke to her husband in a soft, coarse voice: 20

"Get some chairs, why don't you, so somebody can sit down."

"Oh sure," agreed Wilson hurriedly and went toward the little office, mingling immediately with the cement color of the walls. A white ashen dust veiled his dark suit and his pale hair as it veiled everything in the vicinity—except his wife, who moved close to Tom.   25

"I want to see you," said Tom intently. "Get on the next train."

"All right."

"I'll meet you by the news-stand on the lower level."

She nodded and moved away from him just as George Wilson emerged with two chairs from his office door.   30

We waited for her down the road and out of sight. It was a few days before the Fourth of July, and a grey, scrawny Italian child was setting torpedoes in a row along the railroad track.

"Terrible place, isn't it," said Tom, exchanging a frown with Doctor Eckleburg.   35

"Awful."

"It does her good to get away."

"Doesn't her husband object?"

"Wilson? He thinks she goes to see her sister in New York. He's so
40 dumb he doesn't know he's alive."

So Tom Buchanan and his girl and I went up together to New York—
or not quite together, for Mrs. Wilson sat discreetly in another car. Tom
deferred that much to the sensibilities of those East Eggers who might
be on the train.

45 She had changed her dress to a brown figured muslin which stretched
tight over her rather wide hips as Tom helped her to the platform in
New York. At the news-stand she bought a copy of "Town Tattle" and a
moving picture magazine and, in the station drug store, some cold
cream and a small flask of perfume. Upstairs in the solemn echoing
50 drive she let four taxi cabs drive away before she selected a new one,
lavender-colored with grey upholstery, and in this we slid out from the
mass of the station into the glowing sunshine. But immediately she
turned sharply from the window and leaning forward tapped on the
front glass.

55 "I want to get one of those dogs," she said earnestly. "I want to get
one for the apartment. They're nice to have—a dog."

We backed up to a grey old man who bore an absurd resemblance to
John D. Rockefeller. In a basket, swung from his neck, cowered a dozen
very recent puppies of an indeterminate breed.

60 "What kind are they?" asked Mrs. Wilson eagerly as he came to the
taxi window.

"All kinds. What kind do you want, lady?"

"I'd like to get one of those police dogs; I don't suppose you got that
kind?"

---

13 **faintly**: slightly   **surplus** ['sɜːpləs]: more than is needed   13–14 **sensuously**:
(here) in a way that is appealing to the senses   15 **crêpe-de-chine**: soft, thin cloth,
usu. of silk, used for women's blouses, etc.   **facet**: aspect   17 **smoulder**: burn
slowly without flame   19 **flush** (adv): (here) directly   23 **mingle with sth.**: join,
combine with sth.   24 **veil sth.**: hide sth.   24–25 **in the vicinity** (fml): nearby
26 **intently**: full of eager interest   32 **scrawny** (derog): not having much flesh
33 **torpedo**: type of firecracker   43 **defer to sb./sth.**: give way to sb./sth.
45 **muslin**: Musselin   49 **solemn**: (here) very impressive   58 **John D. Rockefeller**
(1839–1937): American billionaire who unified the oil industry into the Standard
Oil Trust   59 **indeterminate** [ˌɪndɪtɜːmɪnət]: (here) unrecognizable

The man peered doubtfully into the basket, plunged in his hand and drew one up, wriggling, by the back of the neck.

"That's no police dog," said Tom.

"No, it's not exactly a po*lice* dog," said the man with disappointment in his voice. "It's more of an airedale." He passed his hand over the brown washrag of a back. "Look at that coat. Some coat. That's a dog that'll never bother you with catching cold." 5

"I think it's cute," said Mrs. Wilson enthusiastically. "How much is it?"

"That dog?" He looked at it admiringly. "That dog will cost you ten dollars." 10

The airedale—undoubtedly there was an airedale concerned in it somewhere though its feet were startlingly white—changed hands and settled down into Mrs. Wilson's lap where she fondled the weather-proof coat with rapture. 15

"Is it a boy or a girl?" she asked delicately.

"That dog? That dog's a boy."

"It's a bitch," said Tom decisively. "Here's your money. Go and buy ten more dogs with it."

We drove over to Fifth Avenue, so warm and soft, almost pastoral, on the summer Sunday afternoon that I wouldn't have been surprised to see a great flock of white sheep turn the corner. 20

"Hold on," I said. "I have to leave you here."

"No, you don't," interposed Tom quickly. "Myrtle'll be hurt if you don't come up to the apartment. Won't you, Myrtle?" 25

"Come on," she urged. "I'll telephone my sister Catherine. She's said to be very beautiful by people who ought to know."

"Well, I'd like to, but——"

We went on, cutting back again over the Park toward the West Hundreds. At 158th Street the cab stopped at one slice in a long white cake of apartment houses. Throwing a regal homecoming glance around the neighborhood, Mrs. Wilson gathered up her dog and her other purchases and went haughtily in. 30

"I'm going to have the McKees come up," she announced as we rose in the elevator. "And of course I got to call up my sister too." 35

The apartment was on the top floor—a small living room, a small dining room, a small bedroom and a bath. The living room was crowded

to the doors with a set of tapestried furniture entirely too large for it so that to move about was to stumble continually over scenes of ladies
40 swinging in the gardens of Versailles. The only picture was an over-enlarged photograph, apparently a hen sitting on a blurred rock. Looked at from a distance however the hen resolved itself into a bonnet and the countenance of a stout old lady beamed down into the room. Several old copies of "Town Tattle" lay on the table together with a copy of
45 "Simon Called Peter" and some of the small scandal magazines of Broadway. Mrs. Wilson was first concerned with the dog. A reluctant elevator boy went for a box full of straw and some milk to which he added on his own initiative a tin of large hard dog biscuits—one of which decomposed apathetically in the saucer of milk all afternoon.
50 Meanwhile Tom brought out a bottle of whiskey from a locked bureau door.

I have been drunk just twice in my life and the second time was that afternoon, so everything that happened has a dim hazy cast over it although until after eight o'clock the apartment was full of cheerful sun.
55 Sitting on Tom's lap Mrs. Wilson called up several people on the telephone; then there were no cigarettes and I went out to buy some at the drug store on the corner. When I came back they had disappeared so I sat down discreetly in the living room and read a chapter of "Simon Called Peter"—either it was terrible stuff or the whiskey distorted things
60 because it didn't make any sense to me.

1 **plunge sth. in**: move sth. downward   2 **wriggle**: make quick and twisting movements   6 **coat**: (here) skin, fur   8 **cute** (AE infml): pretty   13 **startingly**: surprisingly   14 **fondle sth.**: touch sth. gently and lovingly   15 **rapture**: intense delight   20 **Fifth Avenue**: fashionable street in Manhattan   **pastoral** ['pæstərəl]: of or belonging to the countryside   24 **interpose** (fml): interrupt   30 **158th Street**: street in Washington Heights, then a respectable but not fashionable area of Manhattan   **slice**: (here) piece   31 **cake**: (here) shaped mass of sth.   **regal**: royal 33 **haughtily**: arrogantly   38 **tapestried**: decorated with tapestries (= *Gobelins*) 41 **blurred**: unclear   42 **bonnet**: hat tied with strings under the chin   45 "**Simon Called Peter**": popular novel in the 1920s by Robert Keable (1887–1927) about the passions of an army chaplain   49 **decompose**: dissolve   50 **bureau**: desk with drawers   53 **dim, hazy cast**: faint, misty quality   59 **distort sth.**: twist out of its natural shape

Just as Tom and Myrtle—after the first drink Mrs. Wilson and I called each other by our first names—reappeared, company commenced to arrive at the apartment door.

The sister, Catherine, was a slender, worldly girl of about thirty with a solid sticky bob of red hair and a complexion powdered milky white. 5
Her eyebrows had been plucked and then drawn on again at a more rakish angle but the efforts of nature toward the restoration of the old alignment gave a blurred air to her face. When she moved about there was an incessant clicking as innumerable pottery bracelets jingled up and down upon her arms. She came in with such a proprietary haste 10
and looked around so possessively at the furniture that I wondered if she lived here. But when I asked her she laughed immoderately, repeated my question aloud and told me she lived with a girl friend at a hotel.

Mr. McKee was a pale feminine man from the flat below. He had just shaved for there was a white spot of lather on his cheekbone and he was 15
most respectful in his greeting to everyone in the room. He informed me that he was in the "artistic game" and I gathered later that he was a photographer and had made the dim enlargement of Mrs. Wilson's mother which hovered like an ectoplasm on the wall. His wife was shrill, languid, handsome and horrible. She told me with pride that her 20
husband had photographed her a hundred and twenty-seven times since they had been married.

Mrs. Wilson had changed her costume some time before and was now attired in an elaborate afternoon dress of cream-colored chiffon which gave out a continual rustle as she swept about the room. With the 25
influence of the dress her personality had also undergone a change. The intense vitality that had been so remarkable in the garage was converted into impressive hauteur. Her laughter, her gestures, her assertions became more violently affected moment by moment and as she expanded the room grew smaller around her until she seemed to be revolving on a 30
noisy, creaking pivot through the smoky air.

"My dear," she told her sister in a high mincing shout, "most of these fellas will cheat you every time. All they think of is money. I had a woman up here last week to look at my feet and when she gave me the bill you'd of thought she had my appendicitus out." 35

"What was the name of the woman?" asked Mrs. McKee.

"Mrs. Eberhardt. She goes around looking at people's feet in their own homes."

"I like your dress," remarked Mrs. McKee. "I think it's adorable."

40 Mrs. Wilson rejected the compliment by raising her eyebrow in disdain.

"It's just a crazy old thing," she said. "I just slip it on sometimes when I don't care what I look like."

"But it looks wonderful on you, if you know what I mean," pursued 45 Mrs. McKee. "If Chester could only get you in that pose I think he could make something of it."

We all looked in silence at Mrs. Wilson who removed a strand of hair from over her eyes and looked back at us with a brilliant smile. Mr. McKee regarded her intently with his head on one side and then moved 50 his hand back and forth slowly in front of his face.

"I should change the light," he said after a moment. "I'd like to bring out the modelling of the features. And I'd try to get hold of all the back hair."

"I wouldn't think of changing the light," cried Mrs. McKee. "I think 55 it's——"

Her husband said "*Sh!*" and we all looked at the subject again whereupon Tom Buchanan yawned audibly and got to his feet.

"You McKees have something to drink," he said. "Get some more ice and mineral water, Myrtle, before everybody goes to sleep."

60 "I told that boy about the ice." Myrtle raised her eyebrows in despair at the shiftlessness of the lower orders. "These people! You have to keep after them all the time."

---

5 **sticky**: sticking together   **bob**: style of hair that is cut evenly short around the head   **complexion**: natural appearance of the skin, esp. of the face   7 **rakish** ['reɪkɪʃ]: wild   8 **alignment**: arrangement; state   9 **incessant**: continual   **pottery**: *Keramik*   10 **proprietary** [prə'praɪətərɪ]: of an owner   12 **immoderately**: excessively   19 **ectoplasm**: (here) spirit, ghost   20 **languid** ['læŋgwɪd]: lacking energy   24 **be attired in sth**. (fml): wear sth.   28 **hauteur** [hoʊ'tɜː] (fml): arrogance   **assertion** statement   29 **affected**: artificial, pretentious   31 **pivot**: central point on which sth. turns   32 **mincing**: artificial   33 **fella** (non-standard pron): fellow   35 **you'd of …**: you would have …   **appendicitus** (non-standard) = **appendix**: *Blinddarm*   41 **disdain**: contempt   61 **shiftlessness**: laziness

She looked at me and laughed pointlessly. Then she flounced over to the dog, kissed it with ecstasy and swept into the kitchen, implying that a dozen chefs awaited her orders there.

"I've done some nice things out on Long Island," asserted Mr. McKee.   5

Tom looked at him blankly.

"Two of them we have framed downstairs."

"Two what?" demanded Tom.

"Two studies. One of them I call 'Montauk Point—the Gulls,' and the other I call 'Montauk Point—the Sea.' "   10

The sister Catherine sat down beside me on the couch.

"Do you live down on Long Island too?" she inquired.

"I live at West Egg."

"Really? I was down there at a party about a month ago. At a man named Gatsby's. Do you know him?"   15

"I live next door to him."

"Well, they say he's a nephew or a cousin of Kaiser Wilhelm's. That's where all his money comes from."

"Really?"

She nodded.   20

"I'm scared of him. I'd hate to have him get anything on me."

This absorbing information about my neighbor was interrupted by Mrs. McKee's pointing suddenly at Catherine:

"Chester, I think you could do something with *her,*" she broke out, but Mr. McKee only nodded in a bored way and turned his attention to   25
Tom.

"I'd like to do more work on Long Island if I could get the entry. All I ask is that they should give me a start."

"Ask Myrtle," said Tom breaking into a short shout of laughter as Mrs. Wilson entered with a tray. "She'll give you a letter of introduction,   30
won't you, Myrtle?"

"Do what?" she asked startled.

"You'll give McKee a letter of introduction to your husband, so he can do some studies of him." His lips moved silently for a moment as he invented. " 'George B. Wilson at the Gasoline Pump,' or something like   35
that."

Catherine leaned close to me and whispered in my ear:

"Neither of them can stand the person they're married to."

"Can't they?"

40 "Can't *stand* them." She looked at Myrtle and then at Tom. "What I say is, why go on living with them if they can't stand them? If I was them I'd get a divorce and get married to each other right away."

"Doesn't she like Wilson either?"

The answer to this was unexpected. It came from Myrtle who had
45 overheard the question and it was violent and obscene.

"You see?" cried Catherine triumphantly. She lowered her voice again. "It's really his wife that's keeping them apart. She's a Catholic and they don't believe in divorce."

Daisy was not a Catholic and I was a little shocked at the elaborateness
50 of the lie.

"When they do get married," continued Catherine, "they're going west to live for a while until it blows over."

"It'd be more discreet to go to Europe."

"Oh, do you like Europe?" she exclaimed surprisingly. "I just got
55 back from Monte Carlo."

"Really."

"Just last year. I went over there with another girl."

"Stay long?"

"No, we just went to Monte Carlo and back. We went by way of
60 Marseilles. We had over twelve hundred dollars when we started but we got gypped out of it all in two days in the private rooms. We had an awful time getting back, I can tell you. God, how I hated that town!"

The late afternoon sky bloomed in the window for a moment like the blue honey of the Mediterranean—then the shrill voice of Mrs. McKee
65 called me back into the room.

"I almost made a mistake too," she declared vigorously. "I almost married a little kyke who'd been after me for years. I knew he was below

---

1 **flounce**: move in an exaggerated manner   9 **Montauk Point**: eastern tip of Long Island   22 **absorbing**: (here) very interesting   45 **overhear sth.**: hear sth. by chance   49 **elaborateness**: state of being complicated   52 **blow over**: (here) pass away without any serious effects   61 **gyp sb.** [dʒɪp] (sl): cheat sb.   63 **bloom**: (here) glow with colour   67 **kyke** (AE derog sl): Jew

me. Everybody kept saying to me, 'Lucille, that man's way below you!'
But if I hadn't met Chester he'd of got me sure."

"Yes, but listen," said Myrtle Wilson, nodding her head up and down.
"At least you didn't marry him."

"I know I didn't."   5

"Well, I married him," said Myrtle ambiguously. "And that's the
difference between your case and mine."

"Why did you, Myrtle?" demanded Catherine. "Nobody forced you
to."

Myrtle considered.   10

"I married him because I thought he was a gentleman," she said
finally. "I thought he knew something about breeding but he wasn't fit to
lick my shoe."

"You were crazy about him for a while," said Catherine.

"Crazy about him!" cried Myrtle incredulously. "Who said I was crazy   15
about him? I never was any more crazy about him than I was about that
man there."

She pointed suddenly at me and everyone looked at me accusingly. I
tried to show by my expression that I had played no part in her past.

"The only *crazy* I was was when I married him. I knew right away I   20
made a mistake. He borrowed somebody's best suit to get married in
and never even told me about it, and the man came after it one day
when he was out." She looked around to see who was listening: " 'Oh, is
that your suit?' I said. 'This is the first I ever heard about it.' But I gave it
to him and then I lay down and cried to beat the band all afternoon."   25

"She really ought to get away from him," resumed Catherine to me.
"They've been living over that garage for eleven years. And Tom's the
first sweetie she ever had."

The bottle of whiskey—a second one—was now in constant demand
by all present, excepting Catherine who "felt just as good on nothing at   30
all." Tom rang for the janitor and sent him for some celebrated
sandwiches which were a complete supper in themselves. I wanted to
get out and walk eastward toward the park through the soft twilight but
each time I tried to go I became entangled in some wild strident
argument which pulled me back, as if with ropes, into my chair. Yet   35
high over the city our line of yellow windows must have contributed
their share of human secrecy to the casual watcher in the darkening

streets, and I was him too, looking up and wondering. I was within and
without, simultaneously enchanted and repelled by the inexhaustible
40   variety of life.

    Myrtle pulled her chair close to mine and suddenly her warm breath
poured over me the story of her first meeting with Tom.

    "It was on the two little seats facing each other that are always the
last ones left on the train. I was going up to New York to see my sister
45   and spend the night. He had on a dress suit and patent leather shoes
and I couldn't keep my eyes off him but every time he looked at me I
had to pretend to be looking at the advertisement over his head. When
we came into the station he was next to me and his white shirt front
pressed against my arm—and so I told him I'd have to call a policeman
50   but he knew I lied. I was so excited that when I got into a taxi with him
I didn't hardly know I wasn't getting into a subway train. All I kept
thinking about over and over was 'You can't live forever, you can't live
forever.' "

    She turned to Mrs. McKee and the room rang full of her artificial
55   laughter.

    "My dear," she cried, "I'm going to give you this dress as soon as I'm
through with it. I've got to get another one tomorrow. I'm going to make
a list of all the things I've got to get. A massage and a wave and a collar
for the dog and one of those cute little ash trays where you touch a
60   spring, and a wreath with a black silk bow for mother's grave that'll last
all summer. I got to write down a list so I won't forget all the things I got
to do."

    It was nine o'clock—almost immediately afterwards I looked at my
watch and found it was ten. Mr. McKee was asleep on a chair with his
65   fists clenched in his lap, like a photograph of a man of action. Taking

---

6 **ambiguous**: having more than one possible meaning   12 **breeding**: (here) good
manners resulting from upbringing or family background   15 **incredulous**:
showing doubt   25 **to beat the band** (AE sl): with great energy and vigour
30 **excepting**: except   31 **janitor**: person who does routine repairs in a building
34 **entangle oneself in sth.**: involve oneself in sth.   **strident**: loud and harsh
39 **enchant sb.**: fill sb. with great delight   **repel sb.**: cause a feeling of distaste in
sb.   **inexhaustible**: that cannot be used up   45 **dress suit**: man's formal suit for
evening wear   **patent leather**: made of a leather that is hard, glossy and black
58 **wave** (n): hair style with curls

out my handkerchief I wiped from his cheek the remains of the spot of
dried lather that had worried me all the afternoon.

The little dog was sitting on the table looking with blind eyes through
the smoke and from time to time groaning faintly. People disappeared,
reappeared, made plans to go somewhere, and then lost each other,   5
searched for each other, found each other a few feet away. Some time
toward midnight Tom Buchanan and Mrs. Wilson stood face to face
discussing in impassioned voices whether Mrs. Wilson had any right to
mention Daisy's name.

"Daisy! Daisy! Daisy!" shouted Mrs. Wilson. "I'll say it whenever I   10
want to! Daisy! Dai——"

Making a short deft movement Tom Buchanan broke her nose with
his open hand.

Then there were bloody towels upon the bathroom floor and women's
voices scolding, and high over the confusion a long broken wail of pain.   15
Mr. McKee awoke from his doze and started in a daze toward the door.
When he had gone half way he turned around and stared at the scene—
his wife and Catherine scolding and consoling as they stumbled here
and there among the crowded furniture with articles of aid, and the
despairing figure on the couch bleeding fluently and trying to spread a   20
copy of "Town Tattle" over the tapestry scenes of Versailles. Then Mr.
McKee turned and continued on out the door. Taking my hat from the
chandelier I followed.

"Come to lunch some day," he suggested as we groaned down in the
elevator.   25

"Where?"

"Anywhere."

"Keep your hands off the lever," snapped the elevator boy.

"I beg your pardon," said Mr. McKee with dignity. "I didn't know I
was touching it."   30

"All right," I agreed, "I'll be glad to."

… I was standing beside his bed and he was sitting up between the
sheets, clad in his underwear, with a great portfolio in his hands.

"Beauty and the Beast … Loneliness … Old Grocery Horse …
Brook'n Bridge. . . ."   35

Then I was lying half asleep in the cold lower level of the Pennsylvania Station, staring at the morning "Tribune" and waiting for the four o'clock train.

15 **scold**: express anger   16 **in a daze**: in a confused way   23 **chandelier** [ˌʃændəˈlɪə]: *Kronleuchter*   33 **portfolio**: flat case (often made of leather) for carrying loose papers, etc.

Chapter 3

There was music from my neighbor's house through the summer nights. In his blue gardens men and girls came and went like moths among the whisperings and the champagne and the stars. At high tide in the afternoon I watched his guests diving from the tower of his raft or taking the sun on the hot sand of his beach while his two motor boats slit the waters of the Sound, drawing aquaplanes over cataracts of foam. On week-ends his Rolls-Royce became an omnibus, bearing parties to and from the city, between nine in the morning and long past midnight, while his station wagon scampered like a brisk yellow bug to meet all trains. And on Mondays eight servants including an extra gardener toiled all day with mops and scrubbing-brushes and hammers and garden shears, repairing the ravages of the night before.

Every Friday five crates of oranges and lemons arrived from a fruiterer in New York—every Monday these same oranges and lemons left his back door in a pyramid of pulpless halves. There was a machine in the kitchen which could extract the juice of two hundred oranges in half an hour, if a little button was pressed two hundred times by a butler's thumb.

At least once a fortnight a corps of caterers came down with several hundred feet of canvas and enough colored lights to make a Christmas tree of Gatsby's enormous garden. On buffet tables, garnished with glistening hors d'œuvre, spiced baked hams crowded against salads of harlequin designs and pastry pigs and turkeys bewitched to a dark gold. In the main hall a bar with a real brass rail was set up, and stocked with gins and liquors and with cordials so long forgotten that most of his female guests were too young to know one from another.

By seven o'clock the orchestra has arrived—no thin five piece affair but a whole pit full of oboes and trombones and saxophones and viols and cornets and piccolos and low and high drums. The last swimmers have come in from the beach now and are dressing upstairs; the cars from New York are parked five deep in the drive, and already the halls

and salons and verandas are gaudy with primary colors and hair shorn
in strange new ways and shawls beyond the dreams of Castile. The bar
is in full swing and floating rounds of cocktails permeate the garden
35   outside until the air is alive with chatter and laughter and casual
innuendo and introductions forgotten on the spot and enthusiastic
meetings between women who never knew each other's names.

The lights grow brighter as the earth lurches away from the sun and
now the orchestra is playing yellow cocktail music and the opera of
40   voices pitches a key higher. Laughter is easier, minute by minute, spilled
with prodigality, tipped out at a cheerful word. The groups change more
swiftly, swell with new arrivals, dissolve and form in the same breath—
already there are wanderers, confident girls who weave here and there
among the stouter and more stable, become for a sharp, joyous moment
45   the center of a group and then excited with triumph glide on through
the sea-change of faces and voices and color under the constantly
changing light.

Suddenly one of these gypsies in trembling opal seizes a cocktail out
of the air, dumps it down for courage and moving her hands like Frisco
50   dances out alone on the canvas platform. A momentary hush; the
orchestra leader varies his rhythm obligingly for her and there is a burst

---

3 **high tide**: *Hochwasser*   5 **slit sth.**: cut through sth.   6 **cataract**: waterfall
9 **scamper**: run quickly   **brisk**: quick, energetic   **bug**: insect   11 **toil**: work
12 **ravages** (pl): damage   15 **pulpless**: without flesh or juice   20 **canvas**: strong
cloth used for making tents, sails, etc.   21 **garnish sth. with sth. else**: decorate sth.
with sth. else   23 **harlequin** (adj): gaily coloured   **pastry pig**: food with a crust (as
in pies) in the form of a pig   **bewitched**: (here) changed as though by magic
25 **cordial** (n): non-alcoholic drink made of fruit juice   27 **no thin five piece
affair**: not just five musicians   28 **viol** (old use): viola   32 **gaudy** ['gɔːdi]: highly
decorated in a vulgar way   **primary colour**: one of the colours from which all other
colours can be obtained by mixing   **shear sth. – shore – shorn**: cut sth.
33 **shawl**: *Umhängetuch*   34 **in full swing**: very active   **round** (n): number, group
permeate ['pɜːrmieɪt] (fml): spread to every part   36 **innuendo**: hint of sth.
unpleasant   38 **lurch**: move unsteadily forward   39 **yellow**: (here) melancholic
40 **pitch**: become louder   41 **prodigality** [,- - '- - -] (fml): extravagance   42 **swell**:
become larger   43 **weave**: (here) move in a zigzag course   46 **sea-change**:
transformation   48 **gypsy**: (here) wandering person   **opal**: (here) bluish-white
colour of a dress   49 **Frisco = Joe Frisco** (1890?–1958): comedian and dancer who
was credited with inventing the dance called the "black bottom"   51 **obliging**:
willing to help

of chatter as the erroneous news goes around that she is Gilda Gray's understudy from the "Follies." The party has begun.

I believe that on the first night I went to Gatsby's house I was one of the few guests who had actually been invited. People were not invited— they went there. They got into automobiles which bore them out to 5 Long Island and somehow they ended up at Gatsby's door. Once there they were introduced by somebody who knew Gatsby and after that they conducted themselves according to the rules of behavior associated with amusement parks. Sometimes they came and went without having met Gatsby at all, came for the party with a simplicity of heart that was 10 its own ticket of admission.

I had been actually invited. A chauffeur in a uniform of robin's egg blue crossed my lawn early that Saturday morning with a surprisingly formal note from his employer—the honor would be entirely Gatsby's, it said, if I would attend his "little party" that night. He had seen me several 15 times and had intended to call on me long before but a peculiar combination of circumstances had prevented it—signed Jay Gatsby in a majestic hand.

Dressed up in white flannels I went over to his lawn a little after seven and wandered around rather ill-at-ease among swirls and eddies 20 of people I didn't know—though here and there was a face I had noticed on the commuting train. I was immediately struck by the number of young Englishmen dotted about; all well dressed, all looking a little hungry and all talking in low earnest voices to solid and prosperous Americans. I was sure that they were all selling something: bonds or 25 insurance or automobiles. They were, at least, agonizingly aware of the easy money in the vicinity and convinced that it was theirs for a few words in the right key.

As soon as I arrived I made an attempt to find my host but the two or three people of whom I asked his whereabouts stared at me in such an 30 amazed way and denied so vehemently any knowledge of his movements that I slunk off in the direction of the cocktail table—the only place in the garden where a single man could linger without looking purposeless and alone.

I was on my way to get roaring drunk from sheer embarrassment 35 when Jordan Baker came out of the house and stood at the head of the marble steps, leaning a little backward and looking with contemptuous interest down into the garden.

Welcome or not, I found it necessary to attach myself to someone
40 before I should begin to address cordial remarks to the passers-by.

"Hello!" I roared, advancing toward her. My voice seemed unnaturally loud across the garden.

"I thought you might be here," she responded absently as I came up. "I remembered you lived next door to———"

45 She held my hand impersonally, as a promise that she'd take care of me in a minute, and gave ear to two girls in twin yellow dresses who stopped at the foot of the steps.

"Hello!" they cried together. "Sorry you didn't win."

That was for the golf tournament. She had lost in the finals the week
50 before.

"You don't know who we are," said one of the girls in yellow, "but we met you here about a month ago."

"You've dyed your hair since then," remarked Jordan and I started but the girls had moved casually on and her remark was addressed to
55 the premature moon, produced like the supper, no doubt, out of a caterer's basket. With Jordan's slender golden arm resting in mine we descended the steps and sauntered about the garden. A tray of cocktails floated at us through the twilight and we sat down at a table with the two girls in yellow and three men, each one introduced to us as Mr.
60 Mumble.

1 **erroneous** (fml): incorrect; mistaken   **Gilda Gray** (1901?–1959): star of the Ziegfeld Follies, an annual musical revue which ran from 1907 to 1931, who invented the dance called the "shimmy"   2 **understudy**: person who learns the part of another person in a play, in order to take his or her place if necessary   12 **robin's egg blue**: light greenish blue   19 **white flannels**: white flannel trousers and jacket   20 **ill-at ease**: uncomfortable   **swirl**: twisting, whirling movement   **eddy**: current of water, air, etc. moving in a circle against the main current   23 **dot**: (here) be scattered about   26 **agonizing**: painful   28 **in the right key**: spoken to the right people at the right time   30 **whereabouts**: place where a person is 32 **slink – slunk slunk**: move in a quiet, sneaking way   35 **roaring drunk**: completely and noisily drunk   40 **cordial** (adj): friendly   53 **dye sth.**: colour sth. 55 **premature**: (here) not completely visible   56 **caterer**: person who provides for food and service for parties

"Do you come to these parties often?" inquired Jordan of the girl beside her.

"The last one was the one I met you at," answered the girl in an alert, confident voice. She turned to her companion: "Wasn't it for you, Lucille?"   5

It was for Lucille too.

"I like to come," Lucille said. "I never care what I do, so I always have a good time. When I was here last I tore my gown on a chair, and he asked me my name and address—inside of a week I got a package from Croirier's with a new evening gown in it."   10

"Did you keep it?" asked Jordan.

"Sure I did. I was going to wear it tonight, but it was too big in the bust and had to be altered. It was gas blue with lavender beads. Two hundred and sixty-five dollars."

"There's something funny about a fellow that'll do a thing like that,"   15
said the other girl eagerly. "He doesn't want any trouble with *any*body."

"Who doesn't?" I inquired.

"Gatsby. Somebody told me——"

The two girls and Jordan leaned together confidentially.

"Somebody told me they thought he killed a man once."   20

A thrill passed over all of us. The three Mr. Mumbles bent forward and listened eagerly.

"I don't think it's so much *that*," argued Lucille skeptically; "it's more that he was a German spy during the war."

One of the men nodded in confirmation.   25

"I heard that from a man who knew all about him, grew up with him in Germany," he assured us positively.

"Oh no," said the first girl, "it couldn't be that, because he was in the American army during the war." As our credulity switched back to her she leaned forward with enthusiasm. "You look at him sometime when   30
he thinks nobody's looking at him. I'll bet he killed a man."

She narrowed her eyes and shivered. Lucille shivered. We all turned and looked around for Gatsby. It was testimony to the romantic speculation he inspired that there were whispers about him from those who had found little that it was necessary to whisper about in this   35
world.

The first supper—there would be another one after midnight—was now being served and Jordan invited me to join her own party who were spread around a table on the other side of the garden. There were
40 three married couples and Jordan's escort, a persistent undergraduate given to violent innuendo and obviously under the impression that sooner or later Jordan was going to yield him up her person to a greater or lesser degree. Instead of rambling, this party had preserved a dignified homogeneity, and assumed to itself the function of representing the staid
45 nobility of the country-side—East Egg condescending to West Egg, and carefully on guard against its spectroscopic gayety.

"Let's get out," whispered Jordan, after a somehow wasteful and inappropriate half hour. "This is much too polite for me."

We got up and she explained that we were going to find the host—I
50 had never met him, she said, and it was making me uneasy. The undergraduate nodded in a cynical, melancholy way.

The bar, where we glanced first, was crowded but Gatsby was not there. She couldn't find him from the top of the steps, and he wasn't on the veranda. On a chance we tried an important-looking door, and
55 walked into a high Gothic library, panelled with carved English oak, and probably transported complete from some ruin overseas.

A stout, middle-aged man with enormous owl-eyed spectacles was sitting somewhat drunk on the edge of a great table, staring with un-steady concentration at the shelves of books. As we entered he wheeled
60 excitely around and examined Jordan from head to foot.

"What do you think?" he demanded impetuously.

"About what?"

He waved his hand toward the bookshelves.

"About that. As a matter of fact you needn't bother to ascertain. I
65 ascertained. They're real."

"The books?"

---

4 **alert**: lively; attentive   9 **inside of** (AE): within   13 **gas blue**: colour of a gas flame   **bead**: *Perle*   29 **credulity**: tendency to believe too readily   33 **testimony** ['- - - -]: evidence; proo   40 **undergraduate**: student at a university who has not yet received a bachelor's degree   42 **yield sb. sth. up**: (here) surrender sth. to sb. 43 **ramble**: wander   44 **staid** (fml): resisting change; fixed   45 **condescend to sb.**: deal with sb. in a patronizing way   46 **spectroscopic**: brilliant; glittery   59 **wheel around**: turn around   61 **impetuous**: impulsive   65 **ascertain**: find out

He nodded.

"Absolutely real—have pages and everything. I thought they'd be a nice durable cardboard. Matter of fact they're absolutely real. Pages and——Here! Lemme show you."

Taking our skepticism for granted he rushed to the bookcases and returned with Volume One of the "Stoddard Lectures."

"See!" he cried triumphantly. "It's a bona fide piece of printed matter. It fooled me. This fella's a regular Belasco. It's a triumph. What thoroughness! What realism! Knew when to stop too—didn't cut the pages. But what do you want? What do you expect?"

He snatched the book from me and replaced it hastily on its shelf muttering that if one brick was removed the whole library was liable to collapse.

"Who brought you?" he demanded. "Or did you just come? I was brought. Most people were brought."

Jordan looked at him alertly, cheerfully without answering.

"I was brought by a woman named Roosevelt," he continued. "Mrs. Claud Roosevelt. Do you know her? I met her somewhere last night. I've been drunk for about a week now, and I thought it might sober me up to sit in a library."

"Has it?"

"A little bit, I think. I can't tell yet. I've only been here an hour. Did I tell you about the books? They're real. They're——"

"You told us."

We shook hands with him gravely and went back outdoors.

There was dancing now on the canvas in the garden, old men pushing young girls backward in eternal graceless circles, superior couples holding each other tortuously, fashionably and keeping in the corners— and a great number of single girls dancing individualistically or relieving the orchestra for a moment of the burden of the banjo or the traps. By midnight the hilarity had increased. A celebrated tenor had sung in Italian and a notorious contralto had sung in jazz and between the numbers people were doing "stunts" all over the garden while happy vacuous bursts of laughter rose toward the summer sky. A pair of stage "twins"— who turned out to be the girls in yellow—did a baby act in costume and champagne was served in glasses bigger than finger bowls. The moon

had risen higher, and floating in the Sound was a triangle of silver scales,
trembling a little to the stiff, tinny drip of the banjoes on the lawn.

40 I was still with Jordan Baker. We were sitting at a table with a man of
about my age and a rowdy little girl who gave way upon the slightest
provocation to uncontrollable laughter. I was enjoying myself now. I had
taken two finger bowls of champagne and the scene had changed before
my eyes into something significant, elemental and profound.

At a lull in the entertainment the man looked at me and smiled.

45 "Your face is familiar," he said politely. "Weren't you in the Third
Division during the war?"

"Why, yes. I was in the Ninth Machine-Gun Battalion."

"I was in the Seventh Infantry until June nineteen-eighteen. I knew
I'd seen you somewhere before."

50 We talked for a moment about some wet, grey little villages in France.
Evidently he lived in this vicinity for he told me that he had just bought
a hydroplane and was going to try it out in the morning.

"Want to go with me, old sport? Just near the shore along the
Sound."

55 "What time?"

"Any time that suits you best."

It was on the tip of my tongue to ask his name when Jordan looked
around and smiled.

---

3 **Matter of fact**: As a matter of fact   4 **Lemme**: Let me   6 **"Stoddard Lectures"**:
printed speeches etc. of John Lawson Stoddard   7 **bona fide** [ˌbəʊnə ˈfaɪdi]:
authentic   8 **Belasco = David Belasco** (1853–1931): American actor and theatrical
producer famous for the realism of his sets   9 **didn't cut the pages**: the leaves have
not been slit, i.e. the book have never been read   12–13 **liable to do sth.**: likely to
do sth.   25 **gravely**: with dignity; solemnly   27 **graceless**: clumsy; not elegant
28 **tortuously**: *umständlich*   29–30 **relieve sb. of sth.**: take sth. away from sb.
30 **traps** (pl): percussion instruments, e.g. cymbals, bells, etc. attached to a set of
drums   31 **hilarity**: loud laughter; great amusement   32 **notorious**: well-known
for being bad in some way   **contralto**: woman who sings with the lowest female
voice   33 **stunt**: sth. done to attract attention   **vacuous** (fml): senseless, stupid
35 **baby act in costume**: the twin sisters did a performance in which they dressed as
babies and sang, etc.   37 **triangle**: *Dreieck*   38 **tinny**: having a thin metallic sound
drip: (here) the way the music sounds   40 **rowdy** (derog): noisy   43 **elemental**
(fml): powerful; like the forces of nature   44 **lull** (usu. sing): short period of quiet
52 **hydroplane**: seaplane   53 **old sport** (old fashioned BE): fellow

"Having a gay time now?" she inquired.

"Much better." I turned again to my new acquaintance.

"This is an unusual party for me. I haven't even seen the host. I live over there—" I waved my hand at the invisible hedge in the distance, "and this man Gatsby sent over his chauffeur with an invitation."   5

For a moment he looked at me as if he failed to understand.

"I'm Gatsby," he said suddenly.

"What!" I exclaimed. "Oh, I beg your pardon."

"I thought you knew, old sport. I'm afraid I'm not a very good host."

He smiled understandingly—much more than understandingly. It   10 was one of those rare smiles with a quality of eternal reassurance in it, that you may come across four or five times in life. It faced—or seemed to face—the whole external world for an instant, and then concentrated on *you* with an irresistible prejudice in your favor. It understood you just so far as you wanted to be understood, believed in you as you would   15 like to believe in yourself and assured you that it had precisely the impression of you that, at your best, you hoped to convey. Precisely at that point it vanished—and I was looking at an elegant young rough- neck, a year or two over thirty, whose elaborate formality of speech just missed being absurd. Some time before he introduced himself I'd got a   20 strong impression that he was picking his words with care.

Almost at the moment when Mr. Gatsby identified himself a butler hurried toward him with the information that Chicago was calling him on the wire. He excused himself with a small bow that included each of us in turn.   25

"If you want anything just ask for it, old sport," he urged me. "Excuse me. I will rejoin you later."

When he was gone I turned immediately to Jordan— constrained to assure her of my surprise. I had expected that Mr. Gatsby would be a florid and corpulent person in his middle years.   30

"Who is he?" I demanded. "Do you know?"

"He's just a man named Gatsby."

"Where is he from, I mean? And what does he do?"

"Now *you*'re started on the subject," she answered with a wan smile. "Well,—he told me once he was an Oxford man."   35

A dim background started to take shape behind him but at her next remark it faded away.

"However, I don't believe it."

"Why not?"

40   "I don't know," she insisted. "I just don't think he went there."

Something in her tone reminded me of the other girl's "I think he killed a man," and had the effect of stimulating my curiosity. I would have accepted without question the information that Gatsby sprang from the swamps of Louisiana or from the lower East Side of New York.
45   That was comprehensible. But young men didn't—at least in my provincial inexperience I believed they didn't—drift coolly out of nowhere and buy a palace on Long Island Sound.

"Anyhow he gives large parties," said Jordan, changing the subject with an urban distaste for the concrete. "And I like large parties. They're
50   so intimate. At small parties there isn't any privacy."

There was the boom of a bass drum, and the voice of the orchestra leader rang out suddenly above the echolalia of the garden.

"Ladies and gentlemen," he cried. "At the request of Mr. Gatsby we are going to play for you Mr. Vladimir Tostoff's latest work which
55   attracted so much attention at Carnegie Hall last May. If you read the papers you know there was a big sensation." He smiled with jovial condescension and added "Some sensation!" whereupon everybody laughed.

"The piece is known," he concluded lustily, "as 'Vladimir Tostoff's
60   Jazz History of the World.' "

The nature of Mr. Tostoff's composition eluded me, because just as it began my eyes fell on Gatsby, standing alone on the marble steps and looking from one group to another with approving eyes. His tanned skin was drawn attractively tight on his face and his short hair looked as
65   though it were trimmed every day. I could see nothing sinister about him. I wondered if the fact that he was not drinking helped to set him

---

14 **prejudice in sb.'s favor**: judgement to sb.'s advantage   18–19 **roughneck** (sl): crude, tough person   20 **miss sth.**: (here) almost be sth.   28 **constrain** (fml): force sb. to do sth.   30 **florid**: (of a person's face) red in colour   34 **wan**: faint
43 **spring from sth.**: originate from sth.   44 **lower East Side**: poor part of New York City   52 **echolalia** (fml): repetitive noise   55 **Carnegie Hall**: famous concert hall in New York City   57 **condescension**: patronizing behaviour   59 **lustily**: full of vitality   61 **elude sb.**: escape the understanding of sb.   63 **approving**: having a favourable opinion

off from his guests, for it seemed to me that he grew more correct as the fraternal hilarity increased. When the "Jazz History of the World" was over, girls were putting their heads on men's shoulders in a puppyish, convivial way, girls were swooning backward playfully into men's arms, even into groups, knowing that someone would arrest their falls—but no one swooned backward on Gatsby and no French bob touched Gatsby's shoulder and no singing quartets were formed with Gatsby's head for one link.

"I beg your pardon."

Gatsby's butler was suddenly standing beside us.

"Miss Baker?" he inquired. "I beg your pardon but Mr. Gatsby would like to speak to you alone."

"With me?" she exclaimed in surprise.

"Yes, madame."

She got up slowly, raising her eyebrows at me in astonishment, and followed the butler toward the house. I noticed that she wore her evening dress, all her dresses, like sports clothes—there was a jauntiness about her movements as if she had first learned to walk upon golf courses on clean, crisp mornings.

I was alone and it was almost two. For some time confused and intriguing sounds had issued from a long many-windowed room which overhung the terrace. Eluding Jordan's undergraduate who was now engaged in an obstetrical conversation with two chorus girls and who implored me to join him, I went inside.

The large room was full of people. One of the girls in yellow was playing the piano and beside her stood a tall red-haired young lady from a famous chorus, engaged in song. She had drunk a quantity of champagne and during the course of her song she had decided ineptly that everything was very very sad—she was not only singing, she was weeping too. Whenever there was a pause in the song she filled it with gasping broken sobs and then took up the lyric again in a quavering soprano. The tears coursed down her cheeks— not freely, however, for when they came into contact with her heavily beaded eyelashes they assumed an inky color, and pursued the rest of their way in slow black rivulets. A humorous suggestion was made that she sing the notes on her face whereupon she threw up her hands, sank into a chair and went off into a deep vinous sleep.

"She had a fight with a man who says he's her husband," explained a girl at my elbow.

40   I looked around. Most of the remaining women were now having fights with men said to be their husbands. Even Jordan's party, the quartet from East Egg, were rent asunder by dissension. One of the men was talking with curious intensity to a young actress, and his wife after attempting to laugh at the situation in a dignified and indifferent way
45   broke down entirely and resorted to flank attacks—at intervals she appeared suddenly at his side like an angry diamond and hissed "You promised!" into his ear.

The reluctance to go home was not confined to wayward men. The hall was at present occupied by two deplorably sober men and their
50   highly indignant wives. The wives were sympathizing with each other in slightly raised voices.

"Whenever he sees I'm having a good time he wants to go home."

"Never heard anything so selfish in my life."

"We're always the first ones to leave."

55   "So are we."

"Well, we're almost the last tonight," said one of the men sheepishly. "The orchestra left half an hour ago."

In spite of the wives' agreement that such malevolence was beyond credibility, the dispute ended in a short struggle and both wives were
60   lifted kicking into the night.

As I waited for my hat in the hall, the door of the library opened and Jordan Baker and Gatsby came out together. He was saying some last word to her but the eagerness in his manner tightened abruptly into formality as several people approached him to say goodbye.

---

3 **puppyish**: like a puppy (= *Hündchen*)   4 **convivial**: cheerful   **swoon**: act as though one is fainting   6 **French bob**: hairstyle   8 **link**: (here) Bindeglied
17 **jauntiness**: showing cheerfulness and self-confidence   19 **crisp**: dry and cold   22 **elude sb.**: get away from sb.   23 **obstetrical**: (medical) concerned with childbirth   24 **implore sb.**: ask sb. earnestly   28 **inept**: completely unskilful
31 **quaver**: shake; tremble   33 **heavily beaded**: with a lot of make-up   34 **rivulet**: small stream   37 **vinous** (fml): due to wine   42 **rend asunder by dissension**: tear apart due to angry disagreement   45 **resort to sth.**: make use of sth.   **flank attack**: *Flankenangriff*   48 **confined to sb./sth.**: limited to sb./sth.   **wayward**: insistent upon having one's own way   58 **malevolence**: desire to do evil to others   60 **lifted into the night**: lifted up and taken outside

Jordan's party were calling impatiently to her from the porch but she lingered for a moment to shake hands.

"I've just heard the most amazing thing," she whispered. "How long were we in there?"

"Why,—about an hour." 5

"It was—simply amazing," she repeated abstractedly. "But I swore I wouldn't tell it and here I am tantalizing you." She yawned gracefully in my face. "Please come and see me. . . . Phone book. . . . Under the name of Mrs. Sigourney Howard. . . . My aunt. . . ." She was hurrying off as she talked—her brown hand waved a jaunty salute as she melted into 10 her party at the door.

Rather ashamed that on my first appearance I had stayed so late, I joined the last of Gatsby's guests who were clustered around him. I wanted to explain that I'd hunted for him early in the evening and to apologize for not having known him in the garden. 15

"Don't mention it," he enjoined me eagerly. "Don't give it another thought, old sport." The familiar expression held no more familiarity than the hand which reassuringly brushed my shoulder. "And don't forget we're going up in the hydroplane tomorrow morning at nine o'clock." 20

Then the butler, behind his shoulder:

"Philadelphia wants you on the phone, sir."

"All right, in a minute. Tell them I'll be right there. . . . Good night."

"Good night."

"Good night." He smiled—and suddenly there seemed to be a pleas- 25 ant significance in having been among the last to go, as if he had desired it so all the time. "Good night, old sport. . . . Good night."

But as I walked down the steps I saw that the evening was not quite over. Fifty feet from the door a dozen headlights illuminated a bizarre and tumultuous scene. In the ditch beside the road, right side up but 30 violently shorn of one wheel, rested a new coupé which had left Gatsby's drive not two minutes before. The sharp jut of a wall accounted for the detachment of the wheel which was now getting considerable attention from half a dozen curious chauffeurs. However, as they had left their cars blocking the road, a harsh discordant din from those in the rear had 35 been audible for some time and added to the already violent confusion of the scene.

A man in a long duster had dismounted from the wreck and now stood in the middle of the road looking from the car to the tire and from 40 the tire to the observers in a pleasant puzzled way.

"See!" he explained. "It went in the ditch."

The fact was infinitely astonishing to him—and I recognized first the unusual quality of wonder and then the man—it was the late patron of Gatsby's library.

45 "How'd it happen?"

He shrugged his shoulders.

"I know nothing whatever about mechanics," he said decisively.

"But how did it happen? Did you run into the wall?"

"Don't ask me," said Owl Eyes, washing his hands of the whole mat-50 ter. "I know very little about driving—next to nothing. It happened, and that's all I know."

"Well, if you're a poor driver you oughtn't to try driving at night."

"But I wasn't even trying," he explained indignantly. "I wasn't even trying."

55 An awed hush fell upon the bystanders.

"Do you want to commit suicide?"

"You're lucky it was just a wheel! A bad driver and not even *try*ing!"

"You don't understand," explained the criminal. "I wasn't driving. There's another man in the car."

60 The shock that followed this declaration found voice in a sustained "Ah-h-h!" as the door of the coupé swung slowly open. The crowd—it was now a crowd—stepped back involuntarily and when the door had opened wide there was a ghostly pause. Then, very gradually, part by part, a pale dangling individual stepped out of the wreck, pawing tenta-65 tively at the ground with a large uncertain dancing shoe.

---

1 **porch**: covered entrance to a building   6 **abstracted**: thinking of other things
7 **tantalize sb.**: tease sb. by not giving what is desired   13 **cluster around
sb./sth.**: surround sb./sth. closely   16 **enjoin sb.** (fml): urge sb.   32 **jut**: part that
sticks out   **account for sth.**: be the explanation of sth.   33 **detachment**: (here)
state of being broken off   35 **din**: continuing loud confused noise   38 **duster**: light
coat worn by motorists to protect their clothing from road dust   43 **patron**: (here)
visitor   55 **awed hush**: silence due to respect (combined with fear and wonder)
64 **dangle**: (here) stagger   **paw at sth.**: (here) touch sth. with one's feet
64–65 **tentative**: hesitant

Blinded by the glare of the headlights and confused by the incessant groaning of the horns the apparition stood swaying for a moment before he perceived the man in the duster.

"Wha's matter?" he inquired calmly. "Did we run outa gas?"

"Look!"   5

Half a dozen fingers pointed at the amputated wheel—he stared at it for a moment and then looked upward as though he suspected that it had dropped from the sky.

"It came off," someone explained.

He nodded.   10

"At first I din' notice we'd stopped."

A pause. Then taking a long breath and straightening his shoulders he remarked in a determined voice:

"Wonder'ff tell me where there's a gas'line station?"

At least a dozen men, some of them little better off than he was, ex-   15
plained to him that wheel and car were no longer joined by any physical bond.

"Back out," he suggested after a moment. "Put her in reverse."

"But the *wheel's* off!"

He hesitated.   20

"No harm in trying," he said.

The caterwauling horns had reached a crescendo and I turned away and cut across the lawn toward home. I glanced back once. A wafer of a moon was shining over Gatsby's house, making the night fine as before and surviving the laughter and the sound of his still glowing garden. A   25
sudden emptiness seemed to flow now from the windows and the great doors, endowing with complete isolation the figure of the host who stood on the porch, his hand up in a formal gesture of farewell.

Reading over what I have written so far I see I have given the impression that the events of three nights several weeks apart were all that absorbed   30
me. On the contrary, they were merely casual events in a crowded summer and, until much later, they absorbed me infinitely less than my personal affairs.

Most of the time I worked. In the early morning the sun threw my shadow westward as I hurried down the white chasms of lower New   35
York to the Probity Trust. I knew the other clerks and young bond-

salesmen by their first names and lunched with them in dark crowded restaurants on little pig sausages and mashed potatoes and coffee. I even had a short affair with a girl who lived in Jersey City and worked in the
40 accounting department but her brother began throwing mean looks in my direction so when she went on her vacation in July I let it blow quietly away.

I took dinner usually at the Yale Club—for some reason it was the gloomiest event of my day—and then I went upstairs to the library and
45 studied investments and securities for a conscientious hour. There were generally a few rioters around but they never came into the library so it was a good place to work. After that if the night was mellow I strolled down Madison Avenue past the old Murray Hill Hotel and over Thirty-third Street to the Pennsylvania Station.

50 I began to like New York, the racy, adventurous feel of it at night and the satisfaction that the constant flicker of men and women and machines gives to the restless eye. I liked to walk up Fifth Avenue and pick out romantic women from the crowd and imagine that in a few minutes I was going to enter into their lives, and no one would ever
55 know or disapprove. Sometimes, in my mind, I followed them to their apartments on the corners of hidden streets, and they turned and smiled back at me before they faded through a door into warm darkness. At the enchanted metropolitan twilight I felt a haunting loneliness sometimes, and felt it in others—poor young clerks who loitered in front of windows
60 waiting until it was time for a solitary restaurant dinner—young clerks in the dusk, wasting the most poignant moments of night and life.

---

2 **apparition**: (here) ghost-like person   4 **What's matter**: What's the matter   **outa**: out of   11 **din'**: didn't   14 **Wonder'ff**: I wonder if   **gas'line = gasoline**: petrol
22 **caterwaul** ['kætərwɔːl]; make a cat's cry   23 **wafer**: (here) small round piece
27 **endow sb. with sth.**: provide sb. with sth.   35 **chasm** ['kæzəm]: *Schlucht*
36 **probity** (fml): integrity   40 **accounting department**: *Buchhaltung*   43 **Yale Club**: private club for Yale former male students in New York City   45 **securities** (pl): certificates showing who owns stocks, shares, etc.   **conscientious**: (here) filled with great care and attention   46 **rioter**: troublemaker; person out to have fun
47 **mellow**: soft   50 **racy**: lively; vivid   51 **flicker**: sth. that is seen briefly
59 **loiter**: stand about idly   61 **dusk**: time after twilight and before night
poignant: affecting one's feelings deeply

Again at eight o'clock, when the dark lanes of the Forties were five deep with throbbing taxi cabs, bound for the theatre district, I felt a sinking in my heart. Forms leaned together in the taxis as they waited, and voices sang, and there was laughter from unheard jokes, and lighted cigarettes outlined unintelligible gestures inside. Imagining that I, too,   5 was hurrying toward gayety and sharing their intimate excitement, I wished them well.

For a while I lost sight of Jordan Baker, and then in midsummer I found her again. At first I was flattered to go places with her because she was a golf champion and everyone knew her name. Then it was   10 something more. I wasn't actually in love, but I felt a sort of tender curiosity. The bored haughty face that she turned to the world concealed something—most affectations conceal something eventually, even though they don't in the beginning—and one day I found what it was. When we were on a house party together up in Warwick, she left a   15 borrowed car out in the rain with the top down, and then lied about it—and suddenly I remembered the story about her that had eluded me that night at Daisy's. At her first big golf tournament there was a row that nearly reached the newspapers—a suggestion that she had moved her ball from a bad lie in the semi-final round. The thing approached the   20 proportions of a scandal—then died away. A caddy retracted his state-ment and the only other witness admitted that he might have been mistaken. The incident and the name had remained together in my mind.

Jordan Baker instinctively avoided clever shrewd men and now I saw   25 that this was because she felt safer on a plane where any divergence from a code would be thought impossible. She was incurably dishonest. She wasn't able to endure being at a disadvantage, and given this unwillingness I suppose she had begun dealing in subterfuges when she was very young in order to keep that cool insolent smile turned to the   30 world and yet satisfy the demands of her hard jaunty body.

It made no difference to me. Dishonesty in a woman is a thing you never blame deeply—I was casually sorry, and then I forgot. It was on that same house party that we had a curious conversation about driving a car. It started because she passed so close to some workmen that our   35 fender flicked a button on one man's coat.

"You're a rotten driver," I protested. "Either you ought to be more careful or you oughtn't to drive at all."

"I am careful."

40 "No, you're not."

"Well, other people are," she said lightly.

"What's that got to do with it?"

"They'll keep out of my way," she insisted. "It takes two to make an accident."

45 "Suppose you met somebody just as careless as yourself."

"I hope I never will," she answered. "I hate careless people. That's why I like you."

Her grey sun-strained eyes stared straight ahead, but she had deliberately shifted our relations, and for a moment I thought I loved

50 her. But I am slow-thinking and full of interior rules that act as brakes on my desires, and I knew that first I had to get myself definitely out of that tangle back home. I'd been writing letters once a week and signing them "Love, Nick," and all I could think of was how, when that certain girl played tennis, a faint mustache of perspiration appeared on her

55 upper lip. Nevertheless there was a vague understanding that had to be tactfully broken off before I was free.

Everyone suspects himself of at least one of the cardinal virtues, and this is mine: I am one of the few honest people that I have ever known.

---

1 **Forties**: east-west cross streets in midtown Manhattan   2 **throb**: make a persistent sound   5 **unintelligible**: impossible to understand   9 **flattered**: feel honour or pleasure   13 **affectation**: unnatural behaviour; pretence   15 **Warwick**: village outside New York City   18 **row**: dispute   20 **bad lie**: unfavourable position 21 **caddy**: person who carries a golfer's club during a game   **retract sth.** (esp. a statement) (fml): withdraw sth.   25 **shrewd**: having, showing good judgement and common sense   26 **divergence**: action of going in a different direction   27 **code**: set of moral principles governing behaviour   **incurable**: that cannot be corrected 29 **deal in sth.**: concern oneself with sth.   **subterfuge** ['sʌbtərfjuːdʒ]: trick or excuse used to avoid difficulties   30 **insolent** ['ɪnsələnt]: expressing contempt 36 **fender** (AE): wing of a car   **flick sth.**: touch sth. quickly   52 **tangle**: confused mess   57 **suspect sb. of sth.**: mentally accuse sb. of sth.   **cardinal virtue**: *Kardinaltugend*

Chapter 4

On Sunday morning while church bells rang in the villages along shore, the world and its mistress returned to Gatsby's house and twinkled hilariously on his lawn.

"He's a bootlegger," said the young ladies, moving somewhere between his cocktails and his flowers. "One time he killed a man who had ⁄ 5 found out that he was nephew to von Hindenburg and second cousin to the devil. Reach me a rose, honey, and pour me a last drop into that there crystal glass."

Once I wrote down on the empty spaces of a time-table the names of those who came to Gatsby's house that summer. It is an old time-table 10 now, disintegrating at its folds and headed "This schedule in effect July 5th, 1922." But I can still read the grey names and they will give you a better impression than my generalities of those who accepted Gatsby's hospitality and paid him the subtle tribute of knowing nothing whatever about him. 15

From East Egg, then, came the Chester Beckers and the Leeches and a man named Bunsen whom I knew at Yale and Doctor Webster Civet who was drowned last summer up in Maine. And the Hornbeams and the Willie Voltaires and a whole clan named Blackbuck who always gathered in a corner and flipped up their noses like goats at whosoever 20 came near. And the Ismays and the Chrysties (or rather Hubert Auerbach and Mr. Chrystie's wife) and Edgar Beaver whose hair they say turned cotton-white one winter afternoon for no good reason at all.

Clarence Endive was from East Egg, as I remember. He came only once, in white knickerbockers, and had a fight with a bum named Etty 25 in the garden. From farther out on the Island came the Cheadles and the O. R. P. Schraeders and the Stonewall Jackson Abrams of Georgia and the Fishguards and the Ripley Snells. Snell was there three days before he went to the penitentiary, so drunk out on the gravel drive that Mrs. Ulysses Swett's automobile ran over his right hand. The Dancies came 30 too and S. B. Whitebait, who was well over sixty, and Maurice A. Flink and the Hammerheads and Beluga the tobacco importer and Beluga's girls.

From West Egg came the Poles and the Mulreadys and Cecil Roebuck
35 and Cecil Schoen and Gulick, the state senator, and Newton Orchid who controlled Films Par Excellence and Eckhaust and Clyde Cohen and Don S. Schwartze (the son) and Arthur McCarty, all connected with the movies in one way or another. And the Catlips and the Bembergs and G. Earl Muldoon, brother to that Muldoon who afterwards strangled
40 his wife. Da Fontano the promoter came there and Ed Legros and James B. ("Rot-gut") Ferret and the de Jongs and Ernest Lilly—they came to gamble and when Ferret wandered into the garden it meant he was cleaned out and Associated Traction would have to fluctuate profitably next day.

45 A man named Klipspringer was there so often and so long that he became known as "the boarder"—I doubt if he had any other home. Of theatrical people there were Gus Waize and Horace O'Donavan and Lester Myer and George Duckweed and Francis Bull. Also from New York were the Chromes and the Backhyssons and the Dennickers and
50 Russel Betty and the Corrigans and the Kellehers and the Dewars and the Scullys and S. W. Belcher and the Smirkes and the young Quinns, divorced now, and Henry L. Palmetto who killed himself by jumping in front of a subway train in Times Square.

Benny McClenahan arrived always with four girls. They were never
55 quite the same ones in physical person but they were so identical one with another that it inevitably seemed they had been there before. I have forgotten their names—Jaqueline, I think, or else Consuela or Gloria or Judy or June, and their last names were either the melodious names of

---

4 **bootlegger**: person engaged in the illegal sale of alcohol during Prohibition (the period from 1919 to 1933) when there was a federal prohibition law in the USA
6 **Paul von Hindenburg** (1847–1934): president of Germany (1925–1934)
13 **generality**: vague statement   14 **subtle**: not easy to notice   25 **bum** (AE infml): irresponsible person   29 **penitentiary** (AE): federal or state prison   36 **par excellence**: of excellent quality   43 **clean sb. out** (infml): take all of sb.'s money   **fluctuate**: (of stocks and shares) change   46 **boarder**: person who lives at sb. else's house   53 **Times Square**: square in new York City in the theatre district

flowers and months or the sterner ones of the great American capitalists whose cousins, if pressed, they would confess themselves to be.

In addition to all these I can remember that Faustina O'Brien came there at least once and the Baedeker girls and young Brewer who had his nose shot off in the war and Mr. Albrucksburger and Miss Haag, his ⁵ fiancée, and Ardita Fitz-Peters, and Mr. P. Jewett, once head of the American Legion, and Miss Claudia Hip with a man reputed to be her chauffeur, and a prince of something whom we called Duke and whose name, if I ever knew it, I have forgotten.

All these people came to Gatsby's house in the summer.   10

At nine o'clock one morning late in July Gatsby's gorgeous car lurched up the rocky drive to my door and gave out a burst of melody from its three-noted horn. It was the first time he had called on me though I had gone to two of his parties, mounted in his hydroplane, and, at his urgent invitation, made frequent use of his beach.   15

"Good morning, old sport. You're having lunch with me today and I thought we'd ride up together."

He was balancing himself on the dashboard of his car with that re-sourcefulness of movement that is so peculiarly American—that comes, I suppose, with the absence of lifting work or rigid sitting in youth and,   20 even more, with the formless grace of our nervous, sporadic games. This quality was continually breaking through his punctilious manner in the shape of restlessness. He was never quite still; there was always a tapping foot somewhere or the impatient opening and closing of a hand.

He saw me looking with admiration at his car.   25

"It's pretty, isn't it, old sport." He jumped off to give me a better view. "Haven't you ever seen it before?"

I'd seen it. Everybody had seen it. It was a rich cream color, bright with nickel, swollen here and there in its monstrous length with triumphant hatboxes and supper-boxes and tool-boxes, and terraced   30 with a labyrinth of wind-shields that mirrored a dozen suns. Sitting down behind many layers of glass in a sort of green leather conservatory we started to town.

I had talked with him perhaps half a dozen times in the past month and found, to my disappointment, that he had little to say. So my first   35 impression, that he was a person of some undefined consequence, had gradually faded and he had become simply the proprietor of an elaborate roadhouse next door.

And then came that disconcerting ride. We hadn't reached West Egg
40 Village before Gatsby began leaving his elegant sentences unfinished and slapping himself indecisively on the knee of his caramel-colored suit.

"Look here, old sport," he broke out surprisingly. "What's your opinion of me anyhow?"

45 A little overwhelmed I began the generalized evasions which that question deserves.

"Well, I'm going to tell you something about my life," he interrupted. "I don't want you to get a wrong idea of me from all these stories you hear."

50 So he was aware of the bizarre accusations that flavored conversation in his halls.

"I'll tell you God's truth." His right hand suddenly ordered divine retribution to stand by. "I am the son of some wealthy people in the middle-west—all dead now. I was brought up in America but educated
55 at Oxford because all my ancestors have been educated there for many years. It is a family tradition."

He looked at me sideways—and I knew why Jordan Baker had believed he was lying. He hurried the phrase "educated at Oxford," or swallowed it or choked on it as though it had bothered him before. And
60 with this doubt his whole statement fell to pieces and I wondered if there wasn't something a little sinister about him after all.

"What part of the middle-west?" I inquired casually.

"San Francisco."

"I see."

7 **American Legion**: organization of US war veterans, founded in 1919
18 **dashboard**: board below the windscreen of a motor vehicle   18–19 **resource-fulness**: cleverness at finding ways of doing sth.   20 **rigid**: stiff   22 **punctilious** [pʌŋkˈtɪliəs] (fml): very attentive to details of behaviour   30–31 **terraced with sth.**: (here) provided with sth. on different levels   32 **conservatory**: room with glass walls and roof used to protect plants from cold   38 **roadhouse**: restaurant or nightclub on a country road   39 **disconcerting**: causing sb. to feel embarrassed or confused   53 **retribution** (fml): punishment given for causing injury, etc.
63 **San Francisco**: city in the Far West (not in the Mid-West)

"My family all died and I came into a good deal of money."

His voice was solemn as if the memory of that sudden extinction of a clan still haunted him. For a moment I suspected that he was pulling my leg but a glance at him convinced me otherwise.

"After that I lived like a young rajah in all the capitals of Europe— 5 Paris, Venice, Rome—collecting jewels, chiefly rubies, hunting big game, painting a little, things for myself only, and trying to forget something very sad that had happened to me long ago."

With an effort I managed to restrain my incredulous laughter. The very phrases were worn so threadbare that they evoked no image except 10 that of a turbaned "character" leaking sawdust at every pore as he pursued a tiger through the Bois de Boulogne.

"Then came the war, old sport. It was a great relief and I tried very hard to die but I seemed to bear an enchanted life. I accepted a commission as first lieutenant when it began. In the Argonne Forest I took two 15 machine-gun detachments so far forward that there was a half mile gap on either side of us where the infantry couldn't advance. We stayed there two days and two nights, a hundred and thirty men with sixteen Lewis guns, and when the infantry came up at last they found the insignia of three German divisions among the piles of dead. I was promoted to 20 be a major and every Allied government gave me a decoration—even Montenegro, little Montenegro down on the Adriatic Sea!"

Little Montenegro! He lifted up the words and nodded at them— with his smile. The smile comprehended Montenegro's troubled history and sympathized with the brave struggles of the Montenegrin people. It 25 appreciated fully the chain of national circumstances which had elicited this tribute from Montenegro's warm little heart. My incredulity was submerged in fascination now; it was like skimming hastily through a dozen magazines.

He reached in his pocket and a piece of metal, slung on a ribbon, fell 30 into my palm.

"That's the one from Montenegro."

To my astonishment the thing had an authentic look. *Orderi di Danilo*, ran the circular legend, *Montenegro, Nicolas Rex.*

"Turn it." 35

Major Jay Gatsby, I read, *For Valour Extraordinary.*

"Here's another thing I always carry. A souvenir of Oxford days. It was taken in Trinity Quad—the man on my left is now the Earl of Doncaster."

40 It was a photograph of half a dozen young men in blazers loafing in an archway through which were visible a host of spires. There was Gatsby, looking a little, not much, younger—with a cricket bat in his hand.

Then it was all true. I saw the skins of tigers flaming in his palace on 45 the Grand Canal; I saw him opening a chest of rubies to ease, with their crimson-lighted depths, the gnawings of his broken heart.

"I'm going to make a big request of you today," he said, pocketing his souvenirs with satisfaction, "so I thought you ought to know something about me. I didn't want you to think I was just some nobody. You see I 50 usually find myself among strangers because I drift here and there trying to forget the sad thing that happened to me." He hesitated. "You'll hear about it this afternoon."

"At lunch?"

"No, this afternoon. I happened to find out that you're taking Miss 55 Baker to tea."

"Do you mean you're in love with Miss Baker?"

"No, old sport, I'm not. But Miss Baker has kindly consented to speak to you about this matter."

I hadn't the faintest idea what "this matter" was, but I was more 60 annoyed than interested. I hadn't asked Jordan to tea in order to discuss Mr. Jay Gatsby. I was sure the request would be something utterly fan-

---

3–4 **pull sb.'s leg** (infml): make fun of sb.   5 **rajah**: Indian king or prince   6 **big game**: wild animals, e.g. lions, hunted for sport   10 **threadbare**: too often used or too well known to be effective   11 **turbaned**: wearing a turban   12 **Bois de Boulogne**: park in Paris   15 **Argonne Forest**: battle in eastern France between the Aisne and Meuse rivers in late 1918   16 **detachment**: group of soldiers with a special task   26 **elicit sth.** (from sb.) (fml): draw sth. (e.g. information) from sb., usu. with difficulty   27 **incredulity**: feeling of disbelief   28 **skim through sth.**: glance through sth. (e.g. a book) without reading word for word   36 **valour** (fml): bravery (esp. in war)   38 **Trinity Quad**: the quadrangle or courtyard of Trinity College, Oxford University   40 **loaf** (v) (infml): spend time idly   41 **host**: large number   **spire**: *Turmspitze*   45 **Grand Canal**: the main waterway in Venice   46 **gnawing**: continual distress and pain

tastic and for a moment I was sorry I'd ever set foot upon his overpopu-
lated lawn.

He wouldn't say another word. His correctness grew on him as we
neared the city. We passed Port Roosevelt, where there was a glimpse of
red-belted ocean-going ships, and sped along a cobbled slum lined with   5
the dark, undeserted saloons of the faded gilt nineteen-hundreds. Then
the valley of ashes opened out on both sides of us, and I had a glimpse
of Mrs. Wilson straining at the garage pump with panting vitality as we
went by.

With fenders spread like wings we scattered light through half   10
Astoria—only half, for as we twisted among the pillars of the elevated I
heard the familiar "jug-jug-*spat*!" of a motor cycle, and a frantic
policeman rode alongside.

"All right, old sport," called Gatsby. We slowed down. Taking a white
card from his wallet he waved it before the man's eyes.   15

"Right you are," agreed the policeman, tipping his cap. "Know you
next time, Mr. Gatsby. Excuse *me*!"

"What was that?" I inquired. "The picture of Oxford?"

"I was able to do the commissioner a favor once, and he sends me a
Christmas card every year."   20

Over the great bridge, with the sunlight through the girders making
a constant flicker upon the moving cars, with the city rising up across
the river in white heaps and sugar lumps all built with a wish out of
non-olfactory money. The city seen from the Queensboro Bridge is
always the city seen for the first time, in its first wild promise of all the   25
mystery and the beauty in the world.

A dead man passed us in a hearse heaped with blooms, followed by
two carriages with drawn blinds and by more cheerful carriages for
friends. The friends looked out at us with the tragic eyes and short
upper lips of south-eastern Europe and I was glad that the sight of   30
Gatsby's splendid car was included in their somber holiday. As we
crossed Blackwells Island a limousine passed us, driven by a white
chauffeur, in which sat three modish Negroes, two bucks and a girl. I
laughed aloud as the yolks of their eyeballs rolled toward us in haughty
rivalry.   35

"Anything can happen now that we've slid over this bridge," I thought; "anything at all. . . ."

Even Gatsby could happen, without any particular wonder.

Roaring noon. In a well-fanned Forty-Second Street cellar I met Gatsby
40 for lunch. Blinking away the brightness of the street outside my eyes picked him out obscurely in the anteroom, talking to another man.

"Mr. Carraway, this is my friend Mr. Wolfshiem."

A small flat-nosed Jew raised his large head and regarded me with two fine growths of hair which luxuriated in either nostril. After a
45 moment I discovered his tiny eyes in the half darkness.

"—so I took one look at him—" said Mr. Wolfshiem, shaking my hand earnestly, "—and what do you think I did?"

"What?" I inquired politely.

But evidently he was not addressing me for he dropped my hand and
50 covered Gatsby with his expressive nose.

"I handed the money to Katspaugh and I said, 'All right, Katspaugh, don't pay him a penny till he shuts his mouth.' He shut it then and there."

Gatsby took an arm of each of us and moved forward into the
55 restaurant whereupon Mr. Wolfshiem swallowed a new sentence he was starting and lapsed into a somnambulatory abstraction.

3 **grow sb.**: become more established in sb.   5 **cobbled**: paved with cobble stones
(= Kopfsteine)   6 **gilt** (fml): bright like gold   **nineteen-hundreds**: the years
1900–1909   8 **strain**: use all one's power   **pant**: breathe with short quick breaths
11 **elevated** (AE): section of a subway line that runs above ground on trestles
(= Böcken)   12 **frantic**: in an extreme state of emotion   21 **girder**: long strong iron
or steal beam used for building bridges   24 **non-olfactory money**: pun on the Latin
saying "Non olet pecunia" (money does not smell)   27 **hearse** [hɜːs]: vehicle for
carrying a coffin at a funeral   31 **somber**: sad and serious   32 **Blackwells Island**:
island in the East River between Queens and Manhattan, renamed Franklin D.
Roosevelt Island in 1973   33 **buck** (AE sl): young flashy man   34 **yolk**: (here)
central part   39 **roaring**: loud, noisy   **well-fanned**: ventilated   41 **anteroom**:
room leading to a larger or more important room   42 **Wolfshiem**: probably based
on Arnold Rothstein (1882–1928), who was involved in many criminal activities
including the fixing of the World Series in 1919 (cf. annotation for p. 67, l. 32)
44 **luxuriate in sth.**: enjoy sth. as a luxury   **nostril**: *Nasenloch*   56 **lapse into sth.**:
sink gradually into sth.   **somnambulatory** [sɑːmˌnæmbjəˈleɪtəri]: like a
sleepwalker   **abstraction**: absent-mindedness

"Highballs?" asked the headwaiter.

"This is a nice restaurant here," said Mr. Wolfshiem looking at the Presbyterian nymphs on the ceiling. "But I like across the street better!"

"Yes, highballs," agreed Gatsby, and then to Mr. Wolfshiem: "It's too hot over there."   5

"Hot and small—yes," said Mr. Wolfshiem, "but full of memories."

"What place is that?" I asked.

"The old Metropole."

"The old Metropole," brooded Mr. Wolfshiem gloomily. "Filled with faces dead and gone. Filled with friends gone now forever. I can't forget   10
so long as I live the night they shot Rosy Rosenthal there. It was six of us at the table and Rosy had eat and drunk a lot all evening. When it was almost morning the waiter came up to him with a funny look and says somebody wants to speak to him outside. 'All right' says Rosy and begins to get up and I pulled him down in his chair.   15

" 'Let the bastards come in here if they want you, Rosy, but don't you, so help me, move outside this room.'

"It was four o'clock in the morning then and if we'd of raised the blinds we'd of seen daylight."

"Did he go?" I asked innocently.   20

"Sure he went,"—Mr. Wolfshiem's nose flashed at me indignantly—"He turned around in the door and says, 'Don't let that waiter take away my coffee!' Then he went out on the sidewalk and they shot him three times in his full belly and drove away."

"Four of them were electrocuted," I said, remembering.   25

"Five with Becker." His nostrils turned to me in an interested way. "I understand you're looking for a business gonnegtion."

The juxtaposition of these two remarks was startling. Gatsby answered for me.

"Oh, no," he exclaimed, "this isn't the man!"   30

"No?" Mr. Wolfshiem seemed disappointed.

"This is just a friend. I told you we'd talk about that some other time."

"I beg your pardon," said Mr. Wolfshiem. "I had a wrong man."

A succulent hash arrived and Mr. Wolfshiem, forgetting the more   35
sentimental atmosphere of the old Metropole, began to eat with ferocious delicacy. His eyes, meanwhile, roved very slowly all around the room—

he completed the arc by turning to inspect the people directly behind. I
think that, except for my presence, he would have taken one short
40 glance beneath our own table.

"Look here, old sport," said Gatsby leaning toward me. "I'm afraid I
made you a little angry this morning in the car."

There was the smile again, but this time I held out against it.

"I don't like mysteries," I answered. "And I don't understand why
45 you won't come out frankly and tell me what you want. Why has it all
got to come through Miss Baker?"

"Oh, it's nothing underhand," he assured me. "Miss Baker's a great
sportswoman, you know, and she'd never do anything that wasn't all
right."

50 Suddenly he looked at his watch, jumped up and hurried from the
room leaving me with Mr. Wolfshiem at the table.

"He has to telephone," said Mr. Wolfshiem, following him with his
eyes. "Fine fellow, isn't he? Handsome to look at and a perfect
gentleman."

55 "Yes."

"He's an Oggsford man."

"Oh."

"He went to Oggsford College in England. You know Oggsford
College?"

60 "I've heard of it."

"It's one of the most famous colleges in the world."

"Have you known Gatsby for a long time?" I inquired.

"Several years," he answered in a gratified way. "I made the pleasure
of his acquaintance just after the war. But I knew I had discovered a man

---

1 **highball** (AE): liquor, usu. whiskey or brandy, mixed with water, soda water or
ginger ale, etc. and served with ice in a tall glass   3 **Presbyterian**: of a Calvinistic
Protestant denomination   11 **Rosy Rosenthal**: famous gangster murdered in 1912
18–19 **if we'd of raised … we'd of seen** (non-standard): if we had raised … we
would have seen   21 **flash**: move very quickly   27 **gonnegtion** (non-standard
pron): connection   28 **juxtaposition**: placing of people or things which form a
strong contrast side by side   35 **succulent**: juicy and delicious   **hash**: chopped
mixture of cooked meat and vegetables, usu. baked or fried   37 **rove**: look around
38 **arc**: circular movement   43 **hold out (against sth.)**: stand firm against sth.
47 **underhand**: dishonest, illegal   58 **Oggsfold College**: Oxford is a university not
a college

of fine breeding after I talked with him an hour. I said to myself: 'There's the kind of man you'd like to take home and introduce to your mother and sister.' " He paused. "I see you're looking at my cuff buttons."

I hadn't been looking at them, but I did now. They were composed of oddly familiar pieces of ivory.   5

"Finest specimens of human molars," he informed me.

"Well!" I inspected them. "That's a very interesting idea."

"Yeah." He flipped his sleeves up under his coat. "Yeah, Gatsby's very careful about women. He would never so much as look at a friend's wife."   10

When the subject of this instinctive trust returned to the table and sat down, Mr. Wolfshiem drank his coffee with a jerk and got to his feet.

"I have enjoyed my lunch," he said, "and I'm going to run off from you two young men before I outstay my welcome."

"Don't hurry, Meyer," said Gatsby, without enthusiasm. Mr. Wolfshiem   15
raised his hand in a sort of benediction.

"You're very polite but I belong to another generation," he announced solemnly. "You sit here and discuss your sports and your young ladies and your——" He supplied an imaginary noun with another wave of his hand——"As for me, I am fifty years old, and I won't impose myself on   20
you any longer."

As he shook hands and turned away his tragic nose was trembling. I wondered if I had said anything to offend him.

"He becomes very sentimental sometimes," explained Gatsby. "This is one of his sentimental days. He's quite a character around New York—   25
a denizen of Broadway."

"Who is he anyhow—an actor?"

"No."

"A dentist?"

"Meyer Wolfshiem? No, he's a gambler." Gatsby hesitated, then added   30
coolly: "He's the man who fixed the World's Series back in 1919."

"Fixed the World's Series?" I repeated.

The idea staggered me. I remembered of course that the World's Series had been fixed in 1919 but if I had thought of it at all I would have thought of it as a thing that merely *happened,* the end of some   35
inevitable chain. It never occurred to me that one man could start to

play with the faith of fifty million people—with the single-mindedness of a burglar blowing a safe.

40 "How did he happen to do that?" I asked after a minute.

"He just saw the opportunity."

"Why isn't he in jail?"

"They can't get him, old sport. He's a smart man."

I insisted on paying the check. As the waiter brought my change I
45 caught sight of Tom Buchanan across the crowded room.

"Come along with me for a minute," I said. "I've got to say hello to someone."

When he saw us Tom jumped up and took half a dozen steps in our direction.

50 "Where've you been?" he demanded eagerly. "Daisy's furious because you haven't called up."

"This is Mr. Gatsby, Mr. Buchanan."

They shook hands briefly and a strained, unfamiliar look of embarrassment came over Gatsby's face.

55 "How've you been, anyhow?" demanded Tom of me. "How'd you happen to come up this far to eat?"

"I've been having lunch with Mr. Gatsby——"

I turned toward Mr. Gatsby, but he was no longer there.

One October day in nineteen-seventeen—

60 (said Jordan Baker that afternoon, sitting up very straight on a straight chair in the tea-garden at the Plaza Hotel)

—I was walking along from one place to another, half on the sidewalks and half on the lawns. I was happier on the lawns because I had on shoes from England with rubber nobs on the soles that bit into

---

3 **cuff**: *Manschette* 5 **oddly**: strangely 6 **molar**: *Backenzahn* 11 **instinctive**: based on instinct 12 **jerk**: sharp, abrupt movement 15 **outstay sth.**: stay beyond the time of sth. 27 **denizen** (fml): person always to be found in a particular place 32 **fixed the World's Series**: at the end of the baseball season the winning teams from the National League and the American League play to see who wins the championship. In 1919, the Chicago White Sox of the AL were greatly favoured to defeat the Cincinnati Reeds of the NL. The White Sox players were bribed to lose the World's Series. 34 **stagger sb.**: cause sb.'s astonishment or confusion 38 **single-mindedness**: concentration on one aim, purpose, etc. 53 **strained**: tense

the soft ground. I had on a new plaid skirt also that blew a little in the wind and whenever this happened the red, white and blue banners in front of all the houses stretched out stiff and said *tut-tut-tut-tut* in a disapproving way.

The largest of the banners and the largest of the lawns belonged to   5
Daisy Fay's house. She was just eighteen, two years older than me, and by far the most popular of all the young girls in Louisville. She dressed in white and had a little white roadster and all day long the telephone rang in her house and excited young officers from Camp Taylor demanded the privilege of monopolizing her that night, "anyways for an   10
hour!"

When I came opposite her house that morning her white roadster was beside the curb, and she was sitting in it with a lieutenant I had never seen before. They were so engrossed in each other that she didn't see me until I was five feet away.   15

"Hello Jordan," she called unexpectedly. "Please come here."

I was flattered that she wanted to speak to me because of all the older girls I admired her most. She asked me if I was going to the Red Cross and make bandages. I was. Well, then, would I tell them that she couldn't come that day? The officer looked at Daisy while she was speaking, in a   20
way that every young girl wants to be looked at sometime, and because it seemed romantic to me I have remembered the incident ever since. His name was Jay Gatsby and I didn't lay eyes on him again for over four years—even after I'd met him on Long Island I didn't realize it was the same man.   25

That was nineteen-seventeen. By the next year I had a few beaux myself, and I began to play in tournaments, so I didn't see Daisy very often. She went with a slightly older crowd—when she went with anyone at all. Wild rumors were circulating about her—how her mother had found her packing her bag one winter night to go to New York and   30
say goodbye to a soldier who was going overseas. She was effectually prevented, but she wasn't on speaking terms with her family for several weeks. After that she didn't play around with the soldiers any more but only with a few flat-footed, short-sighted young men in town who couldn't get into the army at all.   35

By the next autumn she was gay again, gay as ever. She had a début after the Armistice, and in February she was presumably engaged to a

man from New Orleans. In June she married Tom Buchanan of Chicago
with more pomp and circumstance than Louisville ever knew before.
40   He came down with a hundred people in four private cars and hired a
whole floor of the Seelbach Hotel, and the day before the wedding he
gave her a string of pearls valued at three hundred and fifty thousand
dollars.

I was a bridesmaid. I came into her room half an hour before the
45   bridal dinner and found her lying on her bed as lovely as the June night
in her flowered dress—and as drunk as a monkey. She had a bottle of
sauterne in one hand and a letter in the other.

"'Gratulate me," she muttered. "Never had a drink before but oh,
how I do enjoy it."

50   "What's the matter, Daisy?"

I was scared, I can tell you; I'd never seen a girl like that before.

"Here, dearis." She groped around in a waste-basket she had with her
on the bed and pulled out the string of pearls. "Take 'em downstairs and
give 'em back to whoever they belong to. Tell 'em all Daisy's change' her
55   mine. Say 'Daisy's change' her mine!' "

She began to cry—she cried and cried. I rushed out and found her
mother's maid and we locked the door and got her into a cold bath. She
wouldn't let go of the letter. She took it into the tub with her and
squeezed it up into a wet ball and only let me leave it in the soap dish
60   when she saw that it was coming to pieces like snow.

But she didn't say another word. We gave her spirits of ammonia and
put ice on her forehead and hooked her back into her dress and half an

---

1 **plaid** [plæd]: cloth (usu. with a tartan pattern)   3 **stretch out**: spread out to full
extent   8 **roadster** (old use): small car   10 **monopolize sb.**: (here) have the full
attention of sb.   14 **engrossed in sb./sth.**: fully concentrated on sb./sth.   26 **beau**
[bou] (pl. **beaux** [bouz]) (AE): boyfriend; lover   31 **effectually** (fml): completely
32 **be on speaking terms with sb.**: be willing to talk to sb.   36 **début** ['deɪbju:]:
formal introduction of a young woman (of upper-class background) into society
(normally at a formal ball)   37 **Armistice**: agreement signed on November 11,
1918, that ended World War I   39 **pomp and circumstance**: splendid ceremony
47 **sauterne**: white, relatively sweet table wine   52 **dearis** (AE infml): dear;
darling   **grope around**: search with one's hands   54–55 **Daisy's change' her mine**:
Daisy has changed her mind   61 **spirits of ammonia**: Salmiakgeist   62 **hook sb.
into sth.**: put sb. into a dress and fasten it by means of hooks and eyes (= *Haken*
und *Öse*)

hour later when we walked out of the room the pearls were around her neck and the incident was over. Next day at five o'clock she married Tom Buchanan without so much as a shiver and started off on a three months' trip to the South Seas.

I saw them in Santa Barbara when they came back and I thought I'd never seen a girl so mad about her husband. If he left the room for a minute she'd look around uneasily and say "Where's Tom gone?" and wear the most abstracted expression until she saw him coming in the door. She used to sit on the sand with his head in her lap by the hour rubbing her fingers over his eyes and looking at him with unfathomable delight. It was touching to see them together—it made you laugh in a hushed, fascinated way. That was in August. A week after I left Santa Barbara Tom ran into a wagon on the Ventura road one night and ripped a front wheel off his car. The girl who was with him got into the papers too because her arm was broken—she was one of the chambermaids in the Santa Barbara Hotel.

The next April Daisy had her little girl and they went to France for a year. I saw them one spring in Cannes and later in Deauville and then they came back to Chicago to settle down. Daisy was popular in Chicago, as you know. They moved with a fast crowd, all of them young and rich and wild, but she came out with an absolutely perfect reputation. Perhaps because she doesn't drink. It's a great advantage not to drink among hard-drinking people. You can hold your tongue and, moreover, you can time any little irregularity of your own so that everybody else is so blind that they don't see or care. Perhaps Daisy never went in for amour at all—and yet there's something in that voice of hers. . . .

Well, about six weeks ago, she heard the name Gatsby for the first time in years. It was when I asked you—do you remember?—if you knew Gatsby in West Egg. After you had gone home she came into my room and woke me up and said "What Gatsby?" and when I described him—I was half asleep—she said in the strangest voice that it must be the man she used to know. It wasn't until then that I connected this Gatsby with the officer in her white car.

When Jordan Baker had finished telling all this we had left the Plaza for half an hour and were driving in a Victoria through Central Park. The sun had gone down behind the tall apartments of the movie stars in the

West Fifties and the clear voices of little girls, already gathered like
crickets on the grass, rose through the hot twilight:

> *I'm the Sheik of Araby,*
> *Your love belongs to me.*
> *At night when you're asleep,*
> *Into your tent I'll creep——*

40

"It was a strange coincidence," I said.

"But it wasn't a coincidence at all."

45 "Why not?"

"Gatsby bought that house so that Daisy would be just across the
bay."

Then it had not been merely the stars to which he had aspired on
that June night. He came alive to me, delivered suddenly from the womb
50 of his purposeless splendor.

"He wants to know—" continued Jordan "—if you'll invite Daisy to
your house some afternoon and then let him come over."

The modesty of the demand shook me. He had waited five years and
bought a mansion where he dispensed starlight to casual moths—so
55 that he could "come over" some afternoon to a stranger's garden.

"Did I have to know all this before he could ask such a little thing?"

"He's afraid. He's waited so long. He thought you might be offended.
You see he's a regular tough underneath it all."

Something worried me.

60 "Why didn't he ask you to arrange a meeting?"

"He wants her to see his house," she explained. "And your house is
right next door."

---

3 **without so much as a shiver**: (here) without hesitation for a moment   5 **Santa
Barbara**: town to the north of Los Angeles   9 **by the hour**: for hours
10–11 **unfathomable** (fml): very deep   13 **Ventura road**: highway between Los
Angeles and Santa Barbara   24 **time sth.**: choose the time or moment for sth.
25 **go in for sth.**: indulge in sth.   35 **Victoria**: four-wheeled carriage for two
passengers   38 **cricket**: Grille   39–42 **I'm the Sheik** …: from "The Sheik of
Araby", popular song in 1921, by Ted Snyder, Harry B. Smith and Francis Wheeler
54 **dispense sth. to sb.**: distribute sth. to sb.   **casual**: occasional; careless
58 **regular** (infml): complete   **tough** (n; sl): tough, strong person

"Oh!"

"I think he half expected her to wander into one of his parties, some night," went on Jordan, "but she never did. Then he began asking people casually if they knew her, and I was the first one he found. It was that night he sent for me at his dance, and you should have heard the elaborate way he worked up to it. Of course, I immediately suggested a luncheon in New York—and I thought he'd go mad:

" 'I don't want to do anything out of the way!' he kept saying. 'I want to see her right next door.'

"When I said you were a particular friend of Tom's he started to abandon the whole idea. He doesn't know very much about Tom, though he says he's read a Chicago paper for years just on the chance of catching a glimpse of Daisy's name."

It was dark now and as we dipped under a little bridge I put my arm around Jordan's golden shoulder and drew her toward me and asked her to dinner. Suddenly I wasn't thinking of Daisy and Gatsby any more but of this clean, hard, limited person who dealt in universal skepticism and who leaned back jauntily just within the circle of my arm. A phrase began to beat in my ears with a sort of heady excitement: "There are only the pursued, the pursuing, the busy and the tired."

"And Daisy ought to have something in her life," murmured Jordan to me.

"Does she want to see Gatsby?"

"She's not to know about it. Gatsby doesn't want her to know. You're just supposed to invite her to tea."

We passed a barrier of dark trees, and then the façade of Fifty-Ninth Street, a block of delicate pale light, beamed down into the Park. Unlike Gatsby and Tom Buchanan I had no girl whose disembodied face floated along the dark cornices and blinding signs and so I drew up the girl beside me, tightening my arms. Her wan scornful mouth smiled and so I drew her up again, closer, this time to my face.

14 **dip under sth.**: go below sth.   28 **disembodied**: immaterial; not joined to the body   29 **cornice**: *Gesims*

Chapter 5

When I came home to West Egg that night I was afraid for a moment that my house was on fire. Two o'clock and the whole corner of the peninsula was blazing with light which fell unreal on the shrubbery and made thin, elongating glints upon the roadside wires. Turning a corner I
5   saw that it was Gatsby's house, lit from tower to cellar.

At first I thought it was another party, a wild rout that had resolved itself into "hide-and-go-seek" or "sardines-in-the-box" with all the house thrown open to the game. But there wasn't a sound. Only wind in the trees which blew the wires and made the lights go off and on again as if
10 the house had winked into the darkness. As my taxi groaned away I saw Gatsby walking toward me across his lawn.

"Your place looks like the world's fair," I said.

"Does it?" He turned his eyes toward it absently. "I have been glancing into some of the rooms. Let's go to Coney Island, old sport. In my car."

15 "It's too late."

"Well, suppose we take a plunge in the swimming pool. I haven't made use of it all summer."

"I've got to go to bed."

"All right."

20 He waited, looking at me with suppressed eagerness.

"I talked with Miss Baker," I said after a moment. "I'm going to call up Daisy tomorrow and invite her over here to tea."

"Oh, that's all right," he said carelessly. "I don't want to put you to any trouble."

25 "What day would suit you?"

3 **shrubbery**: area planted with shrubs (= *Büsche, Sträucher*)   4 **elongate sth.**: make sth. longer   **glint** (n): flash of light, esp. as reflected from a hard shiny surface   6 **rout** [raʊt] (n): (here) noisy crowd   7 **hide-and-go-seek**: Versteckspiel **sardines-in-the-box**: Blindekuh   10 **wink**: (here) shine with a light that flashes quickly on and off   12 **world's fair**: international exhibition   14 **Coney Island**: amusement park in Brooklyn

"What day would suit *you*?" he corrected me quickly. "I don't want to put you to any trouble, you see."

"How about the day after tomorrow?"

He considered for a moment. Then, with reluctance:

"I want to get the grass cut," he said. 5

We both looked at the grass—there was a sharp line where my ragged lawn ended and the darker, well-kept expanse of his began. I suspected that he meant my grass.

"There's another little thing," he said uncertainly, and hesitated.

"Would you rather put it off a few days?" I asked. 10

"Oh, it isn't about that. At least——" He fumbled with a series of beginnings. "Why, I thought—why, look here, old sport, you don't make much money, do you?"

"Not very much."

This seemed to reassure him and he continued more confidently. 15

"I thought you didn't, if you'll pardon my—you see, I carry on a little business on the side, a sort of a sideline, you understand. And I thought that if you don't make very much——You're selling bonds, aren't you, old sport?"

"Trying to." 20

"Well, this would interest you. It wouldn't take up much of your time and you might pick up a nice bit of money. It happens to be a rather confidential sort of thing."

I realize now that under different circumstances that conversation might have been one of the crises of my life. But, because the offer was 25 obviously and tactlessly for a service to be rendered, I had no choice except to cut him off there.

"I've got my hands full," I said. "I'm much obliged but I couldn't take on any more work."

"You wouldn't have to do any business with Wolfshiem." Evidently 30 he thought that I was shying away from the "gonnegtion" mentioned at lunch, but I assured him he was wrong. He waited a moment longer, hoping I'd begin a conversation, but I was too absorbed to be responsive, so he went unwillingly home.

The evening had made me light-headed and happy; I think I walked 35 into a deep sleep as I entered my front door. So I don't know whether or not Gatsby went to Coney Island or for how many hours he "glanced into rooms" while his house blazed gaudily on. I called up Daisy from the office next morning and invited her to come to tea.

40 "Don't bring Tom," I warned her.

"What?"

"Don't bring Tom."

"Who is 'Tom'?" she asked innocently.

The day agreed upon was pouring rain. At eleven o'clock a man in a 45 raincoat dragging a lawn-mower tapped at my front door and said that Mr. Gatsby had sent him over to cut my grass. This reminded me that I had forgotten to tell my Finn to come back so I drove into West Egg Village to search for her among soggy white-washed alleys and to buy some cups and lemons and flowers.

50 The flowers were unnecessary, for at two o'clock a greenhouse arrived from Gatsby's, with innumerable receptacles to contain it. An hour later the front door opened nervously and Gatsby in a white flannel suit, silver shirt and gold colored tie hurried in. He was pale and there were dark signs of sleeplessness beneath his eyes.

55 "Is everything all right?" he asked immediately.

"The grass looks fine, if that's what you mean."

"What grass?" he inquired blankly. "Oh, the grass in the yard." He looked out the window at it, but judging from his expression I don't believe he saw a thing.

60 "Looks very good," he remarked vaguely. "One of the papers said they thought the rain would stop about four. I think it was 'The Journal.' Have you got everything you need in the shape of—of tea?"

I took him into the pantry where he looked a little reproachfully at the Finn. Together we scrutinized the twelve lemon cakes from the 65 delicatessen shop.

"Will they do?" I asked.

"Of course, of course! They're fine!" and he added hollowly, "… old sport."

---

7 **expanse**: wide open area   17 **on the side, a sort of sideline** (infml): secretly
26 **render sth.**: give sth.   33 **responsive**: answering warmly or favourably
38 **blaze**: shine brightly   48 **soggy**: very wet   51 **receptacle** (fml): container
64 **scrutinize sth.**: examine sth. carefully

The rain cooled about half past three to a damp mist through which occasional thin drops swam like dew. Gatsby looked with vacant eyes through a copy of Clay's "Economics," starting at the Finnish tread that shook the kitchen floor and peering toward the bleared windows from time to time as if a series of invisible but alarming happenings were 5 taking place outside. Finally he got up and informed me in an uncertain voice that he was going home.

"Why's that?"

"Nobody's coming to tea. It's too late!" He looked at his watch as if there was some pressing demand on his time elsewhere. "I can't wait all 10 day."

"Don't be silly; it's just two minutes to four."

He sat down, miserably, as if I had pushed him, and simultaneously there was the sound of a motor turning into my lane. We both jumped up and, a little harrowed myself, I went out into the yard. 15

Under the dripping bare lilac trees a large open car was coming up the drive. It stopped. Daisy's face, tipped sideways beneath a three-cornered lavender hat, looked out at me with a bright ecstatic smile.

"Is this absolutely where you live, my dearest one?"

The exhilarating ripple of her voice was a wild tonic in the rain. I had 20 to follow the sound of it for a moment, up and down, with my ear alone before any words came through. A damp streak of hair lay like a dash of blue paint across her cheek and her hand was wet with glistening drops as I took it to help her from the car.

"Are you in love with me?" she said low in my ear. "Or why did I 25 have to come alone?"

"That's the secret of Castle Rackrent. Tell your chauffeur to go far away and spend an hour."

"Come back in an hour, Ferdie." Then in a grave murmur, "His name is Ferdie." 30

"Does the gasoline affect his nose?"

"I don't think so," she said innocently. "Why?"

We went in. To my overwhelming surprise the living room was deserted.

"Well, that's funny!" I exclaimed. 35

"What's funny?"

She turned her head as there was a light, dignified knocking at the front door. I went out and opened it. Gatsby, pale as death, with his hands plunged like weights in his coat pockets, was standing in a puddle
40   of water glaring tragically into my eyes.

With his hands still in his coat pockets he stalked by me into the hall, turned sharply as if he were on a wire and disappeared into the living room. It wasn't a bit funny. Aware of the loud beating of my own heart I pulled the door to against the increasing rain.

45   For half a minute there wasn't a sound. Then from the living room I heard a sort of choking murmur and part of a laugh followed by Daisy's voice on a clear artificial note.

"I certainly am awfully glad to see you again."

A pause; it endured horribly. I had nothing to do in the hall so I went
50   into the room.

Gatsby, his hands still in his pockets, was reclining against the mantelpiece in a strained counterfeit of perfect ease, even of boredom. His head leaned back so far that it rested against the face of a defunct mantelpiece clock and from this position his distraught eyes stared
55   down at Daisy who was sitting frightened but graceful on the edge of a stiff chair.

"We've met before," muttered Gatsby. His eyes glanced momentarily at me and his lips parted with an abortive attempt at a laugh. Luckily the clock took this moment to tilt dangerously at the pressure of his head,
60   whereupon he turned and caught it with trembling fingers and set it

---

2 **vacant**: empty   3 **Clay's "Economics"**: introductory book to economics by Henry Clay, published in 1918.   **tread** (sing): manner of walking   4 **peer**: look closely or carefully   **blear sth.**: make sth. dim by tears, water etc.   15 **harrow sb.**: distress sb. greatly   16 **bare**: (here) having lost their leaves   **lilac tree**: *Flieder*
20 **exhilarating**: very exciting   **ripple**: gently rising and falling sound   **tonic** (usu. sing): sth. that makes people feel better   27 **Castle Reckrent**: allusion to an English novel by Maria Edgeworth (1767–1849)   40 **glare**: stare   41 **stalk**: walk with slow stiff strides, esp. in a self-important way   42 **as if he were on a wire**: like a person walking on a tightrope (= Seil)   44 **pull sth. to**: shut sth.   51 **recline against sth.**: lean against sth.   52 **mantelpiece**: shelf above a fireplace   **counterfeit** ['kaʊntərfɪt]: imitation   53 **defunct** (fml): no longer working   54 **distraught** [dɪ'strɔːt]: very worried   58 **abortive**: unsuccessful   59 **tilt**: lean over slightly

back in place. Then he sat down, rigidly, his elbow on the arm of the sofa and his chin in his hand.

"I'm sorry about the clock," he said.

My own face had now assumed a deep tropical burn. I couldn't muster up a single commonplace out of the thousand in my head.

"It's an old clock," I told them idiotically.

I think we all believed for a moment that it had smashed in pieces on the floor.

"We haven't met for many years," said Daisy, her voice as matter-of-fact as it could ever be.

"Five years next November."

The automatic quality of Gatsby's answer set us all back at least another minute. I had them both on their feet with the desperate suggestion that they help me make tea in the kitchen when the demoniac Finn brought it in on a tray.

Amid the welcome confusion of cups and cakes a certain physical decency established itself. Gatsby got himself into a shadow and while Daisy and I talked looked conscientiously from one to the other of us with tense unhappy eyes. However, as calmness wasn't an end in itself I made an excuse at the first possible moment and got to my feet.

"Where are you going?" demanded Gatsby in immediate alarm.

"I'll be back."

"I've got to speak to you about something before you go."

He followed me wildly into the kitchen, closed the door and whispered "Oh, God!" in a miserable way.

"What's the matter?"

"This is a terrible mistake," he said, shaking his head from side to side, "a terrible, terrible mistake."

"You're just embarrassed, that's all," and luckily I added: "Daisy's embarrassed too."

"She's embarrassed?" he repeated incredulously.

"Just as much as you are."

"Don't talk so loud."

"You're acting like a little boy," I broke out impatiently. "Not only that but you're rude. Daisy's sitting in there all alone."

He raised his hand to stop my words, looked at me with unforgettable reproach and opening the door cautiously went back into the other room.

I walked out the back way—just as Gatsby had when he had made
40 his nervous circuit of the house half an hour before—and ran for a huge black knotted tree whose massed leaves made a fabric against the rain. Once more it was pouring and my irregular lawn, well-shaved by Gatsby's gardener, abounded in small muddy swamps and prehistoric marshes. There was nothing to look at from under the tree except
45 Gatsby's enormous house so I stared at it, like Kant at his church steeple, for half an hour. A brewer had built it early in the "period" craze, a decade before, and there was a story that he'd agreed to pay five years' taxes on all the neighboring cottages if the owners would have their roofs thatched with straw. Perhaps their refusal took the heart out of his
50 plan to Found a Family—he went into an immediate decline. His children sold his house with the black wreath still on the door. Americans, while occasionally willing to be serfs, have always been obstinate about being peasantry.

After half an hour the sun shone again and the grocer's automobile
55 rounded Gatsby's drive with the raw material for his servants' dinner—I felt sure he wouldn't eat a spoonful. A maid began opening the upper windows of his house, appeared momentarily in each and, leaning from a large central bay, spat meditatively into the garden. It was time I went back. While the rain continued it had seemed like the murmur of their
60 voices, rising and swelling a little, now and then, with gusts of emotion. But in the new silence I felt that silence had fallen within the house too.

---

5 **muster sth. up**: find sth. within oneself   9–10 **matter-of-fact**: showing no emotion   14 **demoniac** [dɪˈmoʊniæk]: (here) fiercely energetic   41 **massed**: together in a large number   43 **abound in sth.**: have sth. in great numbers
45 **Kant = Immanuel Kant** (1724-1804): German philosopher, who was said to have the habit of looking at a steeple when he was thinking   46 **craze**: sth. that is the fashion for a short time   52 **serf**: *Leibeigene*   53 **obstinate**: refusing to change one's opinion   **peasantry** (sing): poor agricultural workers   58 **bay**: *Erker*   **spit**: *spucken*   **meditative**: absorbed in thought   60 **gust**: outburst

I went in—after making every possible noise in the kitchen short of pushing over the stove—but I don't believe they heard a sound. They were sitting at either end of the couch looking at each other as if some question had been asked or was in the air, and every vestige of embarrassment was gone. Daisy's face was smeared with tears and when I came in she jumped up and began wiping at it with her handkerchief before a mirror. But there was a change in Gatsby that was simply confounding. He literally glowed; without a word or a gesture of exultation a new well-being radiated from him and filled the little room. 5

"Oh, hello, old sport," he said, as if he hadn't seen me for years. I thought for a moment he was going to shake hands. 10

"It's stopped raining."

"Has it?" When he realized what I was talking about, that there were twinkle-bells of sunshine in the room, he smiled like a weather man, like an ecstatic patron of recurrent light, and repeated the news to Daisy. "What do you think of that? It's stopped raining." 15

"I'm glad, Jay." Her throat, full of aching, grieving beauty, told only of her unexpected joy.

"I want you and Daisy to come over to my house," he said. "I'd like to show her around." 20

"You're sure you want me to come?"

"Absolutely, old sport."

Daisy went upstairs to wash her face—too late I thought with humiliation of my towels—while Gatsby and I waited on the lawn.

"My house looks well, doesn't it?" he demanded. "See how the whole front of it catches the light." 25

I agreed that it was splendid.

"Yes." His eyes went over it, every arched door and square tower. "It took me just three years to earn the money that bought it."

"I thought you inherited your money." 30

"I did, old sport," he said automatically, "but I lost most of it in the big panic—the panic of the war."

I think he hardly knew what he was saying, for when I asked him what business he was in he answered "That's my affair," before he realized that it wasn't an appropriate reply. 35

"Oh, I've been in several things," he corrected himself. "I was in the drug business and then I was in the oil business. But I'm not in either one now." He looked at me with more attention. "Do you mean you've been thinking over what I proposed the other night?"

40   Before I could answer, Daisy came out of the house and two rows of brass buttons on her dress gleamed in the sunlight.

"That huge place *there*?" she cried pointing.

"Do you like it?"

"I love it, but I don't see how you live there all alone."

45   "I keep it always full of interesting people, night and day. People who do interesting things. Celebrated people."

Instead of taking the short cut along the Sound we went down to the road and entered by the big postern. With enchanting murmurs Daisy admired this aspect or that of the feudal silhouette against the sky,
50   admired the gardens, the sparkling odor of jonquils and the frothy odor of hawthorn and plum blossoms and the pale gold odor of kiss-me-at-the-gate. It was strange to reach the marble steps and find no stir of bright dresses in and out the door and hear no sound but bird voices in the trees.

55   And inside, as we wandered through Marie Antoinette music-rooms and Restoration salons, I felt that there were guests concealed behind every couch and table, under orders to be breathlessly silent until we had passed through. As Gatsby closed the door of "the Merton College Library" I could have sworn I heard the owl-eyed man break into ghostly
60   laughter.

We went upstairs, through period bedrooms swathed in rose and lavender silk and vivid with new flowers, through dressing rooms and

---

1 **short of**: except   4 **vestige**: trace; small amount   7 **confounding**: puzzling, surprising   8 **exultation**: great happiness   14 **twinkle**: shine with a light that changes constantly from bright to faint   15 **recurrent**: happening often or regularly   17 **grieve** (fml): to feel great sorrow   24 **humiliation**: lowering of self-respect   28 **arch**: curved structure supporting the weigh of sth. above it   37 **drug** (AE): medicine   48 **postern** ['poʊstərn] (old fashioned): side or back entrance 50 **jonquil** ['dʒɑːŋkwɪl]: *Jonquille, Binsennarzisse*   **frothy**: covered with froth or foam   51 **hawthorn**: *Rot-, Weißdorn*   51–52 **kiss-me-at-the-gate**: *Stiefmütterchen* 55 **Marie-Antoinette** (1755-1793): queen of France (1774–1793)   56 **Restoration**: name given to the period following the return of Charles II as king of England in 1660   58 **Merton College**: college of Oxford University   61 **period** (attrib.): (here) according to the fashion of former times   **swathe in sth.**: wrap sth. in several layers of cloth

poolrooms, and bathrooms with sunken baths—intruding into one chamber where a dishevelled man in pajamas was doing liver exercises on the floor. It was Mr. Klipspringer, the "boarder." I had seen him wandering hungrily about the beach that morning. Finally we came to Gatsby's own apartment, a bedroom and a bath and an Adam study, 5 where we sat down and drank a glass of some Chartreuse he took from a cupboard in the wall.

He hadn't once ceased looking at Daisy and I think he revalued everything in his house according to the measure of response it drew from her well-loved eyes. Sometimes, too, he stared around at his 10 possessions in a dazed way as though in her actual and astounding presence none of it was any longer real. Once he nearly toppled down a flight of stairs.

His bedroom was the simplest room of all—except where the dresser was garnished with a toilet set of pure dull gold. Daisy took the brush 15 with delight and smoothed her hair, whereupon Gatsby sat down and shaded his eyes and began to laugh.

"It's the funniest thing, old sport," he said hilariously. "I can't— when I try to——"

He had passed visibly through two states and was entering upon a 20 third. After his embarrassment and his unreasoning joy he was consumed with wonder at her presence. He had been full of the idea so long, dreamed it right through to the end, waited with his teeth set, so to speak, at an inconceivable pitch of intensity. Now, in the reaction, he was running down like an overwound clock. 25

Recovering himself in a minute he opened for us two hulking patent cabinets which held his massed suits and dressing gowns and ties, and his shirts piled like bricks in stacks a dozen high.

"I've got a man in England who buys me clothes. He sends over a selection of things at the beginning of each season, spring and fall." 30

He took out a pile of shirts and began throwing them one by one before us, shirts of sheer linen and thick silk and fine flannel which lost their folds as they fell and covered the table in many-colored disarray. While we admired he brought more and the soft rich heap mounted higher—shirts with stripes and scrolls and plaids in coral and apple 35 green and lavender and faint orange with monograms of Indian blue.

Suddenly with a strained sound Daisy bent her head into the shirts and began to cry stormily.

"They're such beautiful shirts," she sobbed, her voice muffled in the thick folds. "It makes me sad because I've never seen such—such beautiful shirts before."

After the house we were to see the grounds and the swimming pool and the hydroplane and the midsummer flowers—but outside Gatsby's window it began to rain again so we stood in a row looking at the corrugated surface of the Sound.

"If it wasn't for the mist we could see your home across the bay," said Gatsby. "You always have a green light that burns all night at the end of your dock."

Daisy put her arm through his abruptly but he seemed absorbed in what he had just said. Possibly it had occurred to him that the colossal significance of that light had now vanished forever. Compared to the great distance that had separated him from Daisy it had seemed very near to her, almost touching her. It had seemed as close as a star to the moon. Now it was again a green light on a dock. His count of enchanted objects had diminished by one.

I began to walk about the room, examining various indefinite objects in the half darkness. A large photograph of an elderly man in yachting costume attracted me, hung on the wall over his desk.

"Who's this?"

"That? That's Mr. Dan Cody, old sport."

1 **intrude to sth.** (fml): enter sth. (e.g. a place) where one is unwelcome
2 **dishevelled** [dɪˈʃevəld]: untidy   5 **Adam = Robert Adam** (1728–1792) and
James Adam (1730–1794): Scottish brothers who developed the neoclassical style
in Britain   **study** (n): room used for private work or study   6 **Chartreuse**
[ʃɑːrˈtruːz]: green or yellow liqueur made with herbs (after La Grande Chartreuse,
Carthusian monastery in France)   12 **topple**: become unsteady and fall
18 **hilarious**: in a state of amusement   23 **with his teeth set**: prepared to meet sth.
(difficult or unpleasant)   24 **pitch**: (here) degree   26 **hulking** (infml): large and
awkward   26–27 **patent cabinet**: wardrobe designed for one person   33 **disarray**
[ˌdɪsəˈreɪ]: state of being in disorder   35 **scroll**: design in the shape of an "s"
36 **Indian blue**: deep blue   39 **muffle sth.**: make the sound of sth. quieter by
covering it in cloth, etc.   45 **corrugated**: shaped into folds or wrinkles   54 **count**
(usu. sing): total number of things   55 **diminish**: decrease

The name sounded faintly familiar.

"He's dead now. He used to be my best friend years ago."

There was a small picture of Gatsby, also in yachting costume, on the bureau—Gatsby with his head thrown back defiantly—taken apparently when he was about eighteen.   5

"I adore it!" exclaimed Daisy. "The pompadour! You never told me you had a pompadour—or a yacht."

"Look at this," said Gatsby quickly. "Here's a lot of clippings—about you."

They stood side by side examining it. I was going to ask to see the   10
rubies when the phone rang and Gatsby took up the receiver.

"Yes. . . . Well, I can't talk now. . . . I can't talk now, old sport. . . . I said a *small* town. . . . He must know what a small town is. . . . Well, he's no use to us if Detroit is his idea of a small town. . . ."

He rang off.   15

"Come here *quick*!" cried Daisy at the window.

The rain was still falling, but the darkness had parted in the west, and there was a pink and golden billow of foamy clouds above the sea.

"Look at that," she whispered, and then after a moment: "I'd like to just get one of those pink clouds and put you in it and push you   20
around."

I tried to go then, but they wouldn't hear of it; perhaps my presence made them feel more satisfactorily alone.

"I know what we'll do," said Gatsby. "We'll have Klipspringer play the piano."   25

He went out of the room calling "Ewing!" and returned in a few minutes accompanied by an embarrassed, slightly worn young man with shell-rimmed glasses and scanty blonde hair. He was now decently clothed in a "sport-shirt" open at the neck, sneakers and duck trousers of a nebulous hue.   30

"Did we interrupt your exercises?" inquired Daisy politely.

"I was asleep," cried Mr. Klipspringer, in a spasm of embarrassment. "That is, I'd *been* asleep. Then I got up. . . ."

"Klipspringer plays the piano," said Gatsby, cutting him off. "Don't you, Ewing, old sport?"   35

"I don't play well. I don't—I hardly play at all. I'm all out of prac—"

"We'll go downstairs," interrupted Gatsby. He flipped a switch. The grey windows disappeared as the house glowed full of light.

In the music room Gatsby turned on a solitary lamp beside the piano.
40 He lit Daisy's cigarette from a trembling match and sat down with her on a couch far across the room where there was no light save what the gleaming floor bounced in from the hall.

When Klipspringer had played "The Love Nest" he turned around on the bench and searched unhappily for Gatsby in the gloom.
45 "I'm all out of practice, you see. I told you I couldn't play. I'm all out of prac——"

"Don't talk so much, old sport," commanded Gatsby. "Play!"

> *In the morning,*
> *In the evening,*
50 > *Ain't we got fun——*

Outside the wind was loud and there was a faint flow of thunder along the Sound. All the lights were going on in West Egg now; the electric trains, men-carrying, were plunging home through the rain from New York. It was the hour of a profound human change and excitement
55 was generating on the air.

> *One thing's sure and nothing's surer*
> *The rich get richer and the poor get—children.*
> *In the meantime,*
> *In between time——*

4 **defiant**: showing open disobedience   6 **pompadour**: hairstyle in which the hair is combed upward from the forehead to form a high, usu. stiffened wave   8 **clipping**: article cut out of a newspaper, etc.   18 **billow** (old use): large wave   27 **worn**: looking tired and exhausted   28 **shell-rimmed glasses**: Hornbrille   **scanty**: (here) little   29 **duck trousers**: trousers made of a heavy cotton fabric   30 **nebulous**: unclear   **hue** (fml): colour   41 **save** (fml): except   43 "**The Love Nest**": popular song in 1920 by Lewis A. Hirsch and Otto Harbach   48 **In the morning…**: from "Ain't We Got Fun?", popular song in 1921 by Richard A. Whitling, Gus Kahn and Raymond B. Egan

As I went over to say goodbye I saw that the expression of bewil-derment had come back into Gatsby's face, as though a faint doubt had occurred to him as to the quality of his present happiness. Almost five years! There must have been moments even that afternoon when Daisy tumbled short of his dreams—not through her own fault but because of the colossal vitality of his illusion. It had gone beyond her, beyond every-thing. He had thrown himself into it with a creative passion, adding to it all the time, decking it out with every bright feather that drifted his way. No amount of fire or freshness can challenge what a man will store up in his ghostly heart. 10

As I watched him he adjusted himself a little, visibly. His hand took hold of hers and as she said something low in his ear he turned toward her with a rush of emotion. I think that voice held him most with its fluctuating, feverish warmth because it couldn't be over-dreamed—that voice was a deathless song. 15

They had forgotten me but Daisy glanced up and held out her hand; Gatsby didn't know me now at all. I looked once more at them and they looked back at me, remotely, possessed by intense life. Then I went out of the room and down the marble steps into the rain, leaving them there together. 20

5 **tumble short of sth.** (usu. fall short): fail to live up to sth.   8 **deck sth. out**: decorate sth.   11 **adjust oneself**: make oneself better suited to new conditions 13 **rush** (sing): swift movement   14 **feverish**: (here) excited; restless   15 **deathless** (fml): immortal

Chapter 6

About this time an ambitious young reporter from New York arrived one morning at Gatsby's door and asked him if he had anything to say.

"Anything to say about what?" inquired Gatsby politely.

"Why,—any statement to give out."

5   It transpired after a confused five minutes that the man had heard Gatsby's name around his office in a connection which he either wouldn't reveal or didn't fully understand. This was his day off and with laudable initiative he had hurried out "to see."

It was a random shot, and yet the reporter's instinct was right.
10 Gatsby's notoriety, spread about by the hundreds who had accepted his hospitality and so become authorities upon his past, had increased all summer until he fell just short of being news. Contemporary legends such as the "underground pipe-line to Canada" attached themselves to him, and there was one persistent story that he didn't live in a house at
15 all, but in a boat that looked like a house and was moved secretly up and down the Long Island shore. Just why these inventions were a source of satisfaction to James Gatz of North Dakota, isn't easy to say.

James Gatz—that was really, or at least legally, his name. He had changed it at the age of seventeen and at the specific moment that
20 witnessed the beginning of his career—when he saw Dan Cody's yacht drop anchor over the most insidious flat on Lake Superior. It was James Gatz who had been loafing along the beach that afternoon in a torn green jersey and a pair of canvas pants, but it was already Jay Gatsby

---

5 **transpire**: (here) become known   7 **laudable** (fml): deserving praise
9 **random shot**: *Schuss ins Blaue*   10 **notoriety** [ˌnoʊtəˈraɪəti]: fame for being widely known for sth. bad   12 **fall short of sth.**: almost be sth.   13 **underground pipeline to Canada**: one of the myths during Prohibition was that alcohol was being piped into the USA through pipelines   20 **yacht** [jɑːt]   21 **insidious** (fml): (here) dangerous   **flat**: swallow water   **Lake Superior**: largest of the North American Great Lakes

who borrowed a row-boat, pulled out to the *Tuolomee* and informed
Cody that a wind might catch him and break him up in half an hour.

I suppose he'd had the name ready for a long time, even then. His
parents were shiftless and unsuccessful farm people—his imagination
had never really accepted them as his parents at all. The truth was that   5
Jay Gatsby, of West Egg, Long Island, sprang from his Platonic conception
of himself. He was a son of God—a phrase which, if it means anything,
means just that—and he must be about His Father's Business, the service
of a vast, vulgar and meretricious beauty. So he invented just the sort of
Jay Gatsby that a seventeen-year-old boy would be likely to invent, and   10
to this conception he was faithful to the end.

For over a year he had been beating his way along the south shore of
Lake Superior as a clam digger and a salmon fisher or in any other capacity that brought him food and bed. His brown, hardening body lived
naturally through the half-fierce, half-lazy work of the bracing days. He   15
knew women early and since they spoiled him, he became contemptuous
of them, of young virgins because they were ignorant, of the others
because they were hysterical about things which in his overwhelming
self-absorption he took for granted.

But his heart was in a constant, turbulent riot. The most grotesque   20
and fantastic conceits haunted him in his bed at night. A universe of
ineffable gaudiness spun itself out in his brain while the clock ticked on
the wash-stand and the moon soaked with wet light his tangled clothes
upon the floor. Each night he added to the pattern of his fancies until
drowsiness closed down upon some vivid scene with an oblivious em-   25
brace. For a while these reveries provided an outlet for his imagination;
they were a satisfactory hint of the unreality of reality, a promise that the
rock of the world was founded securely on a fairy's wing.

An instinct toward his future glory had led him, some months before,
to the small Lutheran college of St. Olaf in southern Minnesota. He   30
stayed there two weeks, dismayed at its ferocious indifference to the
drums of his destiny, to destiny itself, and despising the janitor's work
with which he was to pay his way through. Then he drifted back to Lake
Superior, and he was still searching for something to do on the day that
Dan Cody's yacht dropped anchor in the shallows along shore.   35

Cody was fifty years old then, a product of the Nevada silver fields,
of the Yukon, of every rush for metal since Seventy-five. The transactions

in Montana copper that made him many times a millionaire found him
physically robust but on the verge of softmindedness, and suspecting
40 this, an infinite number of women tried to separate him from his money.
The none-too-savory ramifications by which Ella Kaye, the newspaper
woman, played Madame de Maintenon to his weakness and sent him to
sea in a yacht, were common knowledge to the turgid journalism of
1902. He had been coasting along all too hospitable shores for five years
45 when he turned up as James Gatz's destiny in Little Girl Bay.

To young Gatz, resting on his oars and looking up at the railed deck,
that yacht represented all the beauty and glamor in the world. I suppose
he smiled at Cody—he had probably discovered that people liked him
when he smiled. At any rate Cody asked him a few questions (one of
50 them elicited the brand new name) and found that he was quick and
extravagantly ambitious. A few days later he took him to Duluth and
bought him a blue coat, six pair of white duck trousers and a yachting
cap. And when the *Tuolomee* left for the West Indies and the Barbary
Coast, Gatsby left too.

55 He was employed in a vague personal capacity—while he remained
with Cody he was in turn steward, mate, skipper, secretary and even

---

4 **shiftless**: lacking ambition   6 **Platonic**: idealistic   8 **His Father's Business**:
reference to "Wist ye not that I must be about my Father's business?" (Bible, Luke ii,
49)   **business**: matter, affair   9 **meretritious** [ˌmerə'trɪʃəs]: apparently attractive
but without any value   13 **clam**: *Venusmuschel*   **digger**: sb. who fishes for clams
15 **bracing**: stimulating   19 **self-absorption**: being interested only in oneself
21 **conceit**: excessive pride in one's powers   23 **soak**: penetrate   **tangle**: cause sth.
to get into a mess   24 **fancy**: fantasy   25 **drowsiness**: state of being half asleep
close down upon sth.: (here) surround sth.   **vivid**: intense, lively   **oblivious**:
having no memory of sth.   26 **reverie**: dream, fantasy   30 **St. Olaf**: college in
Northfield, Minnesota   31 **dismayed**: feeling discouraged   **ferocious**: fierce,
violent   35 **shallows** (pl): *Flachwasser*   37 **Yukon river**: one of the five longest
rivers in Northern British Columbia through Alaska to the Bering Sea   **rush**:
sudden surge of people to a place to mine, etc. for sth., e.g. gold   39 **on the verge
of sth.**: close to sth.   **softmindedness**: *Weichlichkeit*   41 **savory**: pleasant,
enjoyable   **ramifications** (pl.): complex structure   42 **Madame de Maintenon =
Françoise d'Aubigné** (1635–1719): mistress and, from about 1685 on, the second
wife of Louis XIV   43 **turgid** ['tɜːdʒɪd] (derog): pompous and difficult to follow
44 **hospitable**: pleased to welcome guests   46 **oar**: *Riemen*   51 **Duluth**: city and
port on Lake Superior   53–54 **Barbary Coast**: Coast around San Francisco
56 **mate**: *Offizier*   **skipper**: *Kapitän*

jailor, for Dan Cody sober knew what lavish doings Dan Cody drunk might soon be about, and he provided for such contingencies by reposing more and more trust in Gatsby. The arrangement lasted five years during which the boat went three times around the continent. It might have lasted indefinitely, except for the fact that Ella Kaye came on board one night in Boston, and a week later Dan Cody inhospitably died. 5

I remember the portrait of him up in Gatsby's bedroom, a grey, florid man with a hard, empty face—the pioneer debauchee who during one phase of American life brought back to the eastern seaboard the savage violence of the frontier brothel and saloon. It was indirectly due to Cody that Gatsby drank so little. Sometimes in the course of gay parties women used to rub champagne into his hair; for himself he formed the habit of letting liquor alone. 10

And it was from Cody that he inherited money—a legacy of twenty-five thousand dollars. He didn't get it. He never understood the legal device that was used against him but what remained of the millions went intact to Ella Kaye. He was left with his singularly appropriate education; the vague contour of Jay Gatsby had filled out to the substantiality of a man. 15 20

He told me all this very much later, but I've put it down here with the idea of exploding those first wild rumors about his antecedents, which weren't even faintly true. Moreover, he told it to me at a time of confusion, when I had reached the point of believing everything and nothing about him. So I take advantage of this short halt, while Gatsby, so to speak, caught his breath, to clear this set of misconceptions away. 25

It was a halt, too, in my association with his affairs. For several weeks I didn't see him or hear his voice on the phone—mostly I was in New York, trotting around with Jordan and trying to ingratiate myself with her senile aunt— but finally I went over to his house one Sunday afternoon. I hadn't been there two minutes when somebody brought Tom Buchanan in for a drink. I was startled, naturally, but the really surprising thing was that it hadn't happened before. 30

They were a party of three on horseback—Tom and a man named Sloane and a pretty woman in a brown riding habit who had been there previously. 35

"I'm delighted to see you," said Gatsby standing on his porch. "I'm delighted that you dropped in."

As though they cared!

40   "Sit right down. Have a cigarette or a cigar." He walked around the room quickly, ringing bells. "I'll have something to drink for you in just a minute."

He was profoundly affected by the fact that Tom was there. But he would be uneasy anyhow until he had given them something, realizing

45   in a vague way that that was all they came for. Mr. Sloane wanted nothing. A lemonade? No thanks. A little champagne? Nothing at all, thanks. . . . I'm sorry——

"Did you have a nice ride?"

"Very good roads around here."

50   "I suppose the automobiles——"

"Yeah."

Moved by an irresistible impulse Gatsby turned to Tom who had accepted the introduction as a stranger.

"I believe we've met somewhere before, Mr. Buchanan."

55   "Oh, yes," said Tom, gruffly polite but obviously not remembering. "So we did. I remember very well."

"About two weeks ago."

"That's right. You were with Nick here."

"I know your wife," continued Gatsby, almost aggressively.

60   "That so?"

Tom turned to me.

"You live near here, Nick?"

"Next door."

"That so?"

---

1 **sober**: not affected by alcohol   **lavish**: more than enough; generous in giving
2 **contingency**: event that may not occur   2–3 **repose sth. in sb./sth.**: place sth.
(e.g. trust) in sb./sth.   8 **debauchee** [ˌdebɑːˈtʃiː]: immoral person   10 **brothel**:
Bordell   14 **legacy**: money or property left to somebody in a will (= *Testament*)
17 **intact**: complete   18–19 **substantiality**: state of being substantial   21 **explode
sth.**: destroy sth.   **antecedent**: person's ancestor or past life   28 **ingratiate oneself
with sb.**: gain the favour of sb. by doing things that will please him or her
29 **senile**: suffering from mental or physical illness due to age   54 **gruff**: rough in
manner or speech

Mr. Sloane didn't enter into the conversation but lounged back haughtily in his chair; the woman said nothing either— until unexpectedly, after two highballs, she became cordial.

"We'll all come over to your next party, Mr. Gatsby," she suggested. "What do you say?"   5

"Certainly. I'd be delighted to have you."

"Be ver' nice," said Mr. Sloane, without gratitude. "Well—think ought to be starting home."

"Please don't hurry," Gatsby urged them. He had control of himself now and he wanted to see more of Tom. "Why don't you—why don't   10 you stay for supper? I wouldn't be surprised if some other people dropped in from New York."

"You come to supper with *me*," said the lady enthusiastically. "Both of you."

This included me. Mr. Sloane got to his feet.   15

"Come along," he said—but to her only.

"I mean it," she insisted. "I'd love to have you. Lots of room."

Gatsby looked at me questioningly. He wanted to go and he didn't see that Mr. Sloane had determined he shouldn't.

"I'm afraid I won't be able to," I said.   20

"Well, you come," she urged, concentrating on Gatsby.

Mr. Sloane murmured something close to her ear.

"We won't be late if we start now," she insisted aloud.

"I haven't got a horse," said Gatsby. "I used to ride in the army but I've never bought a horse. I'll have to follow you in my car. Excuse me   25 for just a minute."

The rest of us walked out on the porch where Sloane and the lady began an impassioned conversation aside.

"My God, I believe the man's coming," said Tom. "Doesn't he know she doesn't want him?"   30

"She says she does want him."

"She has a big dinner party and he won't know a soul there." He frowned. "I wonder where in the devil he met Daisy. By God, I may be old-fashioned in my ideas, but women run around too much these days to suit me. They meet all kinds of crazy fish."   35

Suddenly Mr. Sloane and the lady walked down the steps and mounted their horses.

"Come on," said Mr. Sloane to Tom. "We're late. We've got to go."
And then to me: "Tell him we couldn't wait, will you?"

40   Tom and I shook hands, the rest of us exchanged a cool nod and they
trotted quickly down the drive, disappearing under the August foliage
just as Gatsby with hat and light overcoat in hand came out the front
door.

Tom was evidently perturbed at Daisy's running around alone, for on the
45   following Saturday night he came with her to Gatsby's party. Perhaps his
presence gave the evening its peculiar quality of oppressiveness—it
stands out in my memory from Gatsby's other parties that summer.
There were the same people, or at least the same sort of people, the
same profusion of champagne, the same many-colored, many-keyed
50   commotion, but I felt an unpleasantness in the air, a pervading harshness
that hadn't been there before. Or perhaps I had merely grown used to it,
grown to accept West Egg as a world complete in itself, with its own
standards and its own great figures, second to nothing because it had no
consciousness of being so, and now I was looking at it again, through
55   Daisy's eyes. It is invariably saddening to look through new eyes at
things upon which you have expended your own powers of adjust-
ment.

They arrived at twilight, and, as we strolled out among the sparkling
hundreds, Daisy's voice was playing murmurous tricks in her throat.

60   "These things excite me *so*," she whispered. "If you want to kiss me
any time during the evening, Nick, just let me know and I'll be glad to
arrange it for you. Just mention my name. Or present a green card. I'm
giving out green—"

"Look around," suggested Gatsby.

65   "I'm looking around. I'm having a marvelous——"

"You must see the faces of many people you've heard about."

Tom's arrogant eyes roamed the crowd.

---

28 **impassioned**: showing strong feelings   35 **suit sb.**: be acceptable to sb.
41 **foliage** ['fəʊliɪdʒ]: leaves of a tree or plant   44 **perturbed**: worried
46 **oppressiveness**: feeling unease   49 **profusion** (sing): large quantity
50 **commotion**: noisy confusion   **pervade**: spread to every part of (sth)
harshness: state of being severe   53 **second to nothing**: unübertroffen
67 **roam**: wander around without any definite aim

"We don't go around very much," he said. "In fact I was just thinking I don't know a soul here."

"Perhaps you know that lady." Gatsby indicated a gorgeous, scarcely human orchid of a woman who sat in state under a white plum tree. Tom and Daisy stared, with that peculiarly unreal feeling that accompanies the recognition of a hitherto ghostly celebrity of the movies. 5

"She's lovely," said Daisy.

"The man bending over her is her director."

He took them ceremoniously from group to group:

"Mrs. Buchanan … and Mr. Buchanan——" After an instant's hesitation he added: "the polo player." 10

"Oh no," objected Tom quickly. "Not me."

But evidently the sound of it pleased Gatsby for Tom remained "the polo player" for the rest of the evening.

"I've never met so many celebrities!" Daisy exclaimed. "I liked that man—what was his name?—with the sort of blue nose." 15

Gatsby identified him, adding that he was a small producer.

"Well, I liked him anyhow."

"I'd a little rather not be the polo player," said Tom pleasantly. "I'd rather look at all these famous people in—in oblivion." 20

Daisy and Gatsby danced. I remember being surprised by his graceful, conservative fox-trot—I had never seen him dance before. Then they sauntered over to my house and sat on the steps for half an hour while at her request I remained watchfully in the garden: "In case there's a fire or a flood," she explained, "or any act of God." 25

Tom appeared from his oblivion as we were sitting down to supper together. "Do you mind if I eat with some people over here?" he said. "A fellow's getting off some funny stuff."

"Go ahead," answered Daisy genially. "And if you want to take down any addresses here's my little gold pencil." … She looked around after a 30 moment and told me the girl was "common but pretty," and I knew that except for the half-hour she'd been alone with Gatsby she wasn't having a good time.

We were at a particularly tipsy table. That was my fault—Gatsby had been called to the phone and I'd enjoyed these same people only two 35 weeks before. But what had amused me then turned septic on the air now.

"How do you feel, Miss Baedeker?"

40 The girl addressed was trying, unsuccessfully, to slump against my shoulder. At this inquiry she sat up and opened her eyes.

"Wha?"

A massive and lethargic woman, who had been urging Daisy to play golf with her at the local club tomorrow, spoke up in Miss Baedeker's defence:

45 "Oh she's all right now. When she's had five or six cocktails she always starts screaming like that. I tell her she ought to leave it alone."

"I do leave it alone," affirmed the accused hollowly.

"We heard you yelling, so I said to Doc Civet here: 'There's somebody that needs your help, Doc.'"

50 "She's much obliged, I'm sure," said another friend, without gratitude. "But you got her dress all wet when you stuck her head in the pool."

"Anything I hate is to get my head stuck in a pool," mumbled Miss Baedeker. "They almost drowned me once over in New Jersey."

"Then you ought to leave it alone," countered Doctor Civet.

55 "Speak for yourself!" cried Miss Baedeker violently. "Your hand shakes. I wouldn't let you operate on me!"

It was like that. Almost the last thing I remember was standing with Daisy and watching the moving picture director and his Star. They were still under the white plum tree and their faces were touching except for

60 a pale thin ray of moonlight between. It occurred to me that he had been very slowly bending toward her all evening to attain this proximity, and even while I watched I saw him stoop one ultimate degree and kiss at her cheek.

"I like her," said Daisy. "I think she's lovely."

65 But the rest offended her—and inarguably, because it wasn't a gesture but an emotion. She was appalled by West Egg, this unprecedented "place" that Broadway had begotten upon a Long Island fishing village—

---

4 **in state**: in rich imposing display   6 **hitherto** (fml): until now   20 **in oblivion**: (here) state of not being known   23 **saunter**: walk in leisurely way   28 **get off some funny stuff**: ein paar Witze, o. ä. loslassen   29 **genial**: kind(ly)   34 **tipsy** (infml): slightly drunk   36 **septic**: toxic; bad   39 **slump**: fall heavily   47 **hollow**: without conviction   54 **counter**: respond (with an opposing view)   61 **proximity** (fml): closeness   62 **stoop**: bend forward and down   66 **appal sb.**: fill sb. with horror   67 **beget sth. – begot/begat – begotten** (old fashioned): cause sth.

appalled by its raw vigor that chafed under the old euphemisms and by the too obtrusive fate that herded its inhabitants along a short cut from nothing to nothing. She saw something awful in the very simplicity she failed to understand.

I sat on the front steps with them while they waited for their car. It was dark here in front: only the bright door sent ten square feet of light volleying out into the soft, black morning. Sometimes a shadow moved against a dressing-room blind above, gave way to another shadow, an indefinite procession of shadows, who rouged and powdered in an invisible glass.

"Who is this Gatsby anyhow?" demanded Tom suddenly. "Some big bootlegger?"

"Where'd you hear that?" I inquired.

"I didn't hear it. I imagined it. A lot of these newly rich people are just big bootleggers, you know."

"Not Gatsby," I said shortly.

He was silent for a moment. The pebbles of the drive crunched under his feet.

"Well, he certainly must have strained himself to get this menagerie together."

A breeze stirred the grey haze of Daisy's fur collar.

"At least they're more interesting than the people we know," she said with an effort.

"You didn't look so interested."

"Well, I was."

Tom laughed and turned to me.

"Did you notice Daisy's face when that girl asked her to put her under a cold shower?"

Daisy began to sing with the music in a husky, rhythmic whisper, bringing out a meaning in each word that it had never had before and would never have again. When the melody rose, her voice broke up sweetly, following it, in a way contralto voices have, and each change tipped out a little of her warm human magic upon the air.

"Lots of people come who haven't been invited," she said suddenly. "That girl hadn't been invited. They simply force their way in and he's too polite to object."

"I'd like to know who he is and what he does," insisted Tom. "And I think I'll make a point of finding out."

"I can tell you right now," she answered. "He owned some drug
40 stores, a lot of drug stores. He built them up himself."

The dilatory limousine came rolling up the drive.

"Good night, Nick," said Daisy.

Her glance left me and sought the lighted top of the steps where "Three o'Clock in the Morning," a neat, sad little waltz of that year, was
45 drifting out the open door. After all, in the very casualness of Gatsby's party, there were romantic possibilities totally absent from her world. What was it up there in the song that seemed to be calling her back inside? What would happen now in the dim incalculable hours? Perhaps some unbelievable guest would arrive, a person infinitely rare and to be
50 marvelled at, some authentically radiant young girl who with one fresh glance at Gatsby, one moment of magical encounter, would blot out those five years of unwavering devotion.

I stayed late that night. Gatsby asked me to wait until he was free and I lingered in the garden until the inevitable swimming party had run up,
55 chilled and exalted, from the black beach, until the lights were extinguished in the guest rooms overhead. When he came down the steps at last, the tanned skin was drawn unusually tight on his face, and his eyes were bright and tired.

"She didn't like it," he said immediately.

60 "Of course she did."

"She didn't like it," he insisted. "She didn't have a good time."

He was silent and I guessed at his unutterable depression.

---

1 **chafe under sth.**: feel impatient with sth.   **euphemism** ['juːfəˌmɪzəm]: use of mild or indirect words instead of more direct ones   2 **obtrusive**: very noticeable; obvious   **herd sb./sth.**: move or drive sb./sth. forward in a particular direction
7 **volley** (v): (here) bounce off   8 **blind**: screen for a window   17 **pebble**: small round stone   41 **dilatory** ['dɪlətəːri] (fml): slow in acting   44 **"Three o'Clock in the Morning"**: waltz by Julian Robledo, with lyrics by Dorothy Terris   50 **marvel at sb./sth.** (fml): admire sb./sth.   51 **blot sth. out**: remove or destroy sth.
52 **unwavering**: unchangeable   55 **chill sb./sth.**: make sb./sth. cold   **exalt sb.** (fml): fill sb. with joy, pride, etc.

"I feel far away from her," he said. "It's hard to make her understand."

"You mean about the dance?"

"The dance?" He dismissed all the dances he had given with a snap of his fingers. "Old sport, the dance is unimportant."   5

He wanted nothing less of Daisy than that she should go to Tom and say: "I never loved you." After she had obliterated three years with that sentence they could decide upon the more practical measures to be taken. One of them was that, after she was free, they were to go back to Louisville and be married from her house—just as if it were   10 five years ago.

"And she doesn't understand," he said despairingly. "She used to be able to understand. We'd sit for hours——"

He broke off and began to walk up and down a desolate path of fruit rinds and discarded favors and crushed flowers.   15

"I wouldn't ask too much of her," I ventured. "You can't repeat the past."

"Can't repeat the past?" he cried incredulously. "Why of course you can!"

He looked around him wildly, as if the past were lurking here in the   20 shadow of his house, just out of reach of his hand.

"I'm going to fix everything just the way it was before," he said, nodding determinedly. "She'll see."

He talked a lot about the past and I gathered that he wanted to recover something, some idea of himself perhaps, that had gone into   25 loving Daisy. His life had been confused and disordered since then, but if he could once return to a certain starting place and go over it all slowly, he could find out what that thing was. . . .

… One autumn night, five years before, they had been walking down the street when the leaves were falling, and they came to a place where   30 there were no trees and the sidewalk was white with moonlight. They stopped here and turned toward each other. Now it was a cool night with that mysterious excitement in it which comes at the two changes of the year. The quiet lights in the houses were humming out into the darkness and there was a stir and bustle among the stars. Out of the   35 corner of his eye Gatsby saw that the blocks of the sidewalk really formed a ladder and mounted to a secret place above the trees—he could climb to it, if he climbed alone, and once there he could suck on the pap of life, gulp down the incomparable milk of wonder.

40   His heart beat faster and faster as Daisy's white face came up to his own. He knew that when he kissed this girl, and forever wed his unutterable visions to her perishable breath, his mind would never romp again like the mind of God. So he waited, listening for a moment longer to the tuning fork that had been struck upon a star. Then he
45   kissed her. At his lips' touch she blossomed for him like a flower and the incarnation was complete.

Through all he said, even through his appalling sentimentality, I was reminded of something—an elusive rhythm, a fragment of lost words, that I had heard somewhere a long time ago. For a moment a phrase
50   tried to take shape in my mouth and my lips parted like a dumb man's, as though there was more struggling upon them than a wisp of startled air. But they made no sound and what I had almost remembered was uncommunicable forever.

7 **obliterate sth.**: destroy sth. completely   15 **rind** [raɪnd]: hard outer skin of some fruits   **discard sth.**: throw sth. away   **favor** (AE): small decorative but worthless gift or party object   16 **venture** (fml): dare to say   20 **lurk**: be hidden
35 **stir** (n): slight movement   **bustle**: excited activity   39 **pap**: nipple   **gulp sth. down**: swallow sth. quickly or greedily   41–42 **wed sth. to sth. else** (fml): unite sth. to sth. else   42 **perishable**: likely to go bad or die   43 **romp**: play in a lively way   44 **tuning fork**: *Stimmgabel*   48 **elusive**: difficult to remember   51 **wisp**: small streak or amount   **startle**: (here) start or move against one's will

Chapter 7

It was when curiosity about Gatsby was at its highest that the lights in his house failed to go on one Saturday night—and, as obscurely as it had begun, his career as Trimalchio was over.

Only gradually did I become aware that the automobiles which turned expectantly into his drive stayed for just a minute and then drove sulkily away. Wondering if he were sick I went over to find out—an unfamiliar butler with a villainous face squinted at me suspiciously from the open door.

"Is Mr. Gatsby sick?"

"Nope." After a pause he added "sir" in a dilatory, grudging way.

"I hadn't seen him around and I was rather worried. Tell him Mr. Carraway came over."

"Who?" he demanded rudely.

"Carraway."

"Carraway. All right, I'll tell him."

Abruptly he slammed the door.

My Finn informed me that Gatsby had dismissed every servant in his house a week ago and replaced them with half a dozen others who never went into West Egg Village to be bribed by the tradesmen, but ordered moderate supplies over the telephone. The grocery boy reported that the kitchen looked like a pigsty and the general opinion in the village was that the new people weren't servants at all.

Next day Gatsby called me on the phone.

"Going away?" I inquired.

"No, old sport."

"I hear you fired all your servants."

"I wanted somebody who wouldn't gossip. Daisy comes over quite often—in the afternoons."

So the whole caravansary had fallen in like a card house at the disapproval in her eyes.

"They're some people Wolfshiem wanted to do something for. They're all brothers and sisters. They used to run a small hotel."

"I see."

He was calling up at Daisy's request—would I come to lunch at her
35 house tomorrow? Miss Baker would be there. Half an hour later Daisy herself telephoned and seemed relieved to find that I was coming. Something was up. And yet I couldn't believe that they would choose this occasion for a scene—especially for the rather harrowing scene that Gatsby had outlined in the garden.

40 The next day was broiling, almost the last, certainly the warmest, of the summer. As my train emerged from the tunnel into sunlight, only the hot whistles of the National Biscuit Company broke the simmering hush at noon. The straw seats of the car hovered on the edge of combustion; the woman next to me perspired delicately for a while into
45 her white shirtwaist and then, as her newspaper dampened under her fingers, lapsed despairingly into deep heat with a desolate cry. Her pocket-book slapped to the floor.

"Oh, my!" she gasped.

I picked it up with a weary bend and handed it back to her holding
50 it at arm's length and by the extreme tip of the corners to indicate that I had no designs upon it—but every one near by, including the woman, suspected me just the same.

"Hot!" said the conductor to familiar faces. "Some weather! … Hot! … Hot! … Hot! … Is it hot enough for you? Is it hot? Is it …?"

3 **Trimalchio**: central character in the Roman satire *Satyricon* by Gaius Petronius Arbiter (died 66 AD), of which "Trimalchio's Dinner" is the best-known. Trimalchio is a wealthy man who held a gigantic banquet for the leading people of Rome. Petronius used the banquet to attack many of the leading figures of Rome.   6 **sulky**: being silent or unsociable as a result of bad temper or resentment   7 **villainous** ['vɪlənəs]: dangerous-looking   **squint at sb.**: look at sb. with eyes partly shut
10 **nope** (sl): no   **grudging**: unwilling   19 **bribe sb.**: give sb. sth. (esp. money) to make him or her do sth.   29 **caravansary** [kærə'vænsəriː]: kind of oriental inn with large central court, where caravans stop for the night   38 **harrowing**: very distressing   39 **outline sth.**: give a general idea of sth.   40 **broil**: become very hot   43 **hush**: silence   **hover**: remain in an uncertain state   44 **combustion**: process of burning   45 **shirtwaist** (AE): woman's shirt   46 **lapse into sth.**: sink gradually into sth.   47 **pocket-book** (AE): wallet, handbag   49 **weary**: exhausted; tired

My commutation ticket came back to me with a dark stain from his hand. That anyone should care in this heat whose flushed lips he kissed, whose head made damp the pajama pocket over his heart!

… Through the hall of the Buchanans' house blew a faint wind, carrying the sound of the telephone bell out to Gatsby and me as we waited at the door.

"The master's body!" roared the butler into the mouthpiece. "I'm sorry Madame but we can't furnish it—it's far too hot to touch this noon!"

What he really said was "Yes. . . . Yes. . . . I'll see."

He set down the receiver and came toward us, glistening slightly, to take our stiff straw hats.

"Madame expects you in the salon!" he cried, needlessly indicating the direction. In this heat every extra gesture was an affront to the common store of life.

The room, shadowed well with awnings, was dark and cool. Daisy and Jordan lay upon an enormous couch, like silver idols, weighing down their own white dresses against the singing breeze of the fans.

"We can't move," they said together.

Jordan's fingers, powdered white over their tan, rested for a moment in mine.

"And Mr. Thomas Buchanan, the athlete?" I inquired.

Simultaneously I heard his voice, gruff, muffled, husky, at the hall telephone.

Gatsby stood in the center of the crimson carpet and gazed around with fascinated eyes. Daisy watched him and laughed her sweet exciting laugh; a tiny gust of powder rose from her bosom into the air.

"The rumor is," whispered Jordan, "that that's Tom's girl on the telephone."

We were silent. The voice in the hall rose high with annoyance. "Very well then, I won't sell you the car at all. . .-. I'm under no obligations to you at all. . . . And as for your bothering me about it at lunch time I won't stand that at all!"

"Holding down the receiver," said Daisy cynically.

"No, he's not," I assured her. "It's a bona fide deal. I happen to know about it."

Tom flung open the door, blocked out its space for a moment with his thick body, and hurried into the room.

"Mr. Gatsby!" He put out his broad, flat hand with well-concealed
40   dislike. "I'm glad to see you, sir. . . . Nick. . . ."

"Make us a cold drink," cried Daisy.

As he left the room again she got up and went over to Gatsby, and pulled his face down, kissing him on the mouth.

"You know I love you," she murmured.
45   "You forget there's a lady present," said Jordan.

Daisy looked around doubtfully.

"You kiss Nick too."

"What a low, vulgar girl!"

"I don't care!" cried Daisy and began to clog on the brick fireplace.
50   Then she remembered the heat and sat down guiltily on the couch just as a freshly laundered nurse leading a little girl came into the room.

"Bles-sed pre-cious," she crooned, holding out her arms. "Come to your own mother that loves you."

The child, relinquished by the nurse, rushed across the room and
55   rooted shyly into her mother's dress.

"The Bles-sed pre-cious! Did mother get powder on your old yellowy hair? Stand up now and say How-de-do."

Gatsby and I in turn leaned down and took the small reluctant hand. Afterward he kept looking at the child with surprise. I don't think he
60   had ever really believed in its existence before.

"I got dressed before luncheon," said the child, turning eagerly to Daisy.

"That's because your mother wanted to show you off." Her face bent into the single wrinkle of the small white neck. "You dream, you. You
65   absolute little dream."

---

1 **commutation ticket** (AE): ticket which covers a certain number of journeys or period of time   2 **flushed**: filled with emotion   8 **furnish sth.**: supply sth.
11 **glisten** ['glɪsn]: (esp. of wet surfaces) shine brightly   16 **awning**: canvas fixed above a door or a window and stretched out to keep out the rain or the sun
49 **clog**: (here) make the sound of clogs (= Holzschuhe)   **fireplace**: (here) area in front of the fireplace   51 **launder** (fml): wash and iron   52 **croon**: hum, sing or speak gently and softly   54 **relinquish sb./sth.** (fml): cease to hold sb./sth.; release sb./sth.

"Yes," admitted the child calmly. "Aunt Jordan's got on a white dress too."

"How do you like mother's friends?" Daisy turned her around so that she faced Gatsby. "Do you think they're pretty?"

"Where's Daddy?"   5

"She doesn't look like her father," explained Daisy. "She looks like me. She's got my hair and shape of the face."

Daisy sat back upon the couch. The nurse took a step forward and held out her hand.

"Come Pammy."   10

"Goodbye, sweetheart!"

With a reluctant backward glance the well-disciplined child held to her nurse's hand and was pulled out the door, just as Tom came back, preceding four gin rickeys that clicked full of ice.

Gatsby took up his drink.   15

"They certainly look cool," he said, with visible tension.

We drank in long greedy swallows.

"I read somewhere that the sun's getting hotter every year," said Tom genially. "It seems that pretty soon the earth's going to fall into the sun— or wait a minute—it's just the opposite—the sun's getting colder every   20
year.

"Come outside," he suggested to Gatsby. "I'd like you to have a look at the place."

I went with them out to the veranda. On the green Sound, stagnant in the heat, one small sail crawled slowly toward the fresher sea. Gatsby's   25
eyes followed it momentarily; he raised his hand and pointed across the bay.

"I'm right across from you."

"So you are."

Our eyes lifted over the rosebeds and the hot lawn and the weedy   30
refuse of the dog days along shore. Slowly the white wings of the boat moved against the blue cool limit of the sky. Ahead lay the scalloped ocean and the abounding blessed isles.

"There's sport for you," said Tom, nodding. "I'd like to be out there with him for about an hour."   35

We had luncheon in the dining room, darkened, too, against the heat, and drank down nervous gayety with the cold ale.

"What'll we do with ourselves this afternoon," cried Daisy, "and the day after that, and the next thirty years?"

40 "Don't be morbid," Jordan said. "Life starts all over again when it gets crisp in the fall."

"But it's so hot," insisted Daisy, on the verge of tears. "And everything's so confused. Let's all go to town!"

Her voice struggled on through the heat, beating against it, moulding
45 its senselessness into forms.

"I've heard of making a garage out of a stable," Tom was saying to Gatsby, "but I'm the first man who ever made a stable out of a garage."

"Who wants to go to town?" demanded Daisy insistently. Gatsby's eyes floated toward her. "Ah," she cried, "you look so cool."

50 Their eyes met, and they stared together at each other, alone in space. With an effort she glanced down at the table.

"You always look so cool," she repeated.

She had told him that she loved him, and Tom Buchanan saw. He was astounded. His mouth opened a little and he looked at Gatsby and
55 then back at Daisy as if he had just recognized her as someone he knew a long time ago.

"You resemble the advertisement of the man," she went on innocently. "You know the advertisement of the man——"

"All right," broke in Tom quickly, "I'm perfectly willing to go to town.
60 Come on—we're all going to town."

He got up, his eyes still flashing between Gatsby and his wife. No one moved.

"Come on!" His temper cracked a little. "What's the matter anyhow? If we're going to town, let's start."

65 His hand, trembling with his effort at self control, bore to his lips the last of his glass of ale. Daisy's voice got us to our feet and out on to the blazing gravel drive.

14 **rickey**: drink made of soda water, lime juice, sugar and liquor, esp. gin
24 **stagnant**: showing no activity   30 **weedy**: overgrown with weeds (= *Unkraut*)
31 **refuse** ['refjuːs]: waste or worthless material   **dog days**: hot, uncomfortable days
in July and August   32 **scalloped**: with a series of curves along the surface
41 **crisp**: hard, dry and easily broken   54 **astound sb.**: overcome sb. with surprise
and shock   57 **you resemble … man**: possibly an allusion to the Arrow Collar
advertisement of the time, which showed a classically handsome man

"Are we just going to go?" she objected. "Like this? Aren't we going to let anyone smoke a cigarette first?"

"Everybody smoked all through lunch."

"Oh, let's have fun," she begged him. "It's too hot to fuss."

He didn't answer. 5

"Have it your own way," she said. "Come on Jordan."

They went upstairs to get ready while we three men stood there shuffling the hot pebbles with our feet. A silver curve of the moon hovered already in the western sky. Gatsby started to speak, changed his mind, but not before Tom wheeled and faced him expectantly. 10

"Pardon me?"

"Have you got your stables here?" asked Gatsby with an effort.

"About a quarter of a mile down the road."

"Oh."

A pause. 15

"I don't see the idea of going to town," broke out Tom savagely. "Women get these notions in their heads——"

"Shall we take anything to drink?" called Daisy from an upper window.

"I'll get some whiskey," answered Tom. He went inside. 20

Gatsby turned to me rigidly:

"I can't say anything in his house, old sport."

"She's got an indiscreet voice," I remarked. "It's full of——"

I hesitated.

"Her voice is full of money," he said suddenly. 25

That was it. I'd never understood before. It was full of money—that was the inexhaustible charm that rose and fell in it, the jingle of it, the cymbals' song of it. . . . High in a white palace the king's daughter, the golden girl. . . .

Tom came out of the house wrapping a quart bottle in a towel, followed 30
by Daisy and Jordan wearing small tight hats of metallic cloth and carrying light capes over their arms.

"Shall we all go in my car?" suggested Gatsby. He felt the hot green leather of the seat. "I ought to have left it in the shade."

"Is it standard shift?" demanded Tom. 35

"Yes."

"Well, you take my coupé and let me drive your car to town."

The suggestion was distasteful to Gatsby.

"I don't think there's much gas," he objected.

40 "Plenty of gas," said Tom boisterously. He looked at the gauge. "And if it runs out I can stop at a drug store. You can buy anything at a drug store nowadays."

A pause followed this apparently pointless remark. Daisy looked at Tom frowning and an indefinable expression, at once definitely unfamiliar 45 and vaguely recognizable, as if I had only heard it described in words, passed over Gatsby's face.

"Come on, Daisy," said Tom, pressing her with his hand toward Gatsby's car. "I'll take you in this circus wagon."

He opened the door but she moved out from the circle of his arm.

50 "You take Nick and Jordan. We'll follow you in the coupé."

She walked close to Gatsby, touching his coat with her hand. Jordan and Tom and I got into the front seat of Gatsby's car, Tom pushed the unfamiliar gears tentatively and we shot off into the oppressive heat leaving them out of sight behind.

55 "Did you see that?" demanded Tom.

"See what?"

He looked at me keenly, realizing that Jordan and I must have known all along.

"You think I'm pretty dumb, don't you?" he suggested. "Perhaps I 60 am, but I have a—almost a second sight, sometimes, that tells me what to do. Maybe you don't believe that, but science——"

He paused. The immediate contingency overtook him, pulled him back from the edge of the theoretical abyss.

"I've made a small investigation of this fellow," he continued. "I could 65 have gone deeper if I'd known——"

"Do you mean you've been to a medium?" inquired Jordan humorously.

"What?" Confused, he stared at us as we laughed. "A medium?"

1 **object**: protest   4 **fuss**: worry about small things   8 **shuffle sth.**: move sth. about with one's feet while standing or sitting   23 **indiscreet**: lacking tact; careless   30 **quart**: ca. 1.14 litres   35 **standard shift**: usual gear lever (= *Gangschaltung*)   40 **gauge** [geɪdʒ]: instrument for measuring the amount or level of sth.   44–45 **at once … and**: at the same time   63 **abyss**: *Abgrund*

"About Gatsby."

"About Gatsby! No, I haven't. I said I'd been making a small investigation of his past."

"And you found he was an Oxford man," said Jordan helpfully.

"An Oxford man!" He was incredulous. "Like hell he is! He wears a 5 pink suit."

"Nevertheless he's an Oxford man."

"Oxford, New Mexico," snorted Tom contemptuously, "or something like that."

"Listen, Tom. If you're such a snob why did you invite him to lunch?" 10 demanded Jordan crossly.

"Daisy invited him; she knew him before we were married—God knows where!"

We were all irritable now with the fading ale and, aware of it, we drove for a while in silence. Then as Doctor T. J. Eckleburg's faded eyes 15 came into sight down the road I remembered Gatsby's caution about gasoline.

"We've got enough to get us to town," said Tom.

"But there's a garage right here," objected Jordan. "I don't want to get stalled in this baking heat." 20

Tom threw on both brakes impatiently and we slid to an abrupt dusty stop under Wilson's sign. After a moment the proprietor emerged from the interior of his establishment and gazed hollow-eyed at the car.

"Let's have some gas!" cried Tom roughly. "What do you think we stopped for—to admire the view?" 25

"I'm sick," said Wilson without moving. "I been sick all day."

"What's the matter?"

"I'm all run down."

"Well, shall I help myself?" Tom demanded. "You sounded well enough on the phone." 30

With an effort Wilson left the shade and support of the doorway and, breathing hard, unscrewed the cap of the tank. In the sunlight his face was green.

"I didn't mean to interrupt your lunch," he said. "But I need money pretty bad and I was wondering what you were going to do with your 35 old car."

"How do you like this one?" inquired Tom. "I bought it last week."

"It's a nice yellow one," said Wilson, as he strained at the handle.
"Like to buy it?"

40 "Big chance," Wilson smiled faintly. "No, but I could make some money on the other."

"What do you want money for all of a sudden?"

"I've been here too long. I want to get away. My wife and I want to go west."

45 "Your wife does!" exclaimed Tom, startled.

"She's been talking about it for ten years." He rested for a moment against the pump, shading his eyes. "And now she's going whether she wants to or not. I'm going to get her away."

The coupé flashed by us with a flurry of dust and the flash of a
50 waving hand.

"What do I owe you?" demanded Tom harshly.

"I just got wised up to something funny the last two days," remarked Wilson. "That's why I want to get away. That's why I been bothering you about the car."

55 "What do I owe you?"

"Dollar twenty."

The relentless beating heat was beginning to confuse me and I had a bad moment there before I realized that so far his suspicions hadn't alighted on Tom. He had discovered that Myrtle had some sort of life
60 apart from him in another world and the shock had made him physically sick. I stared at him and then at Tom, who had made a parallel discovery less than an hour before—and it occurred to me that there was no difference between men, in intelligence or race, so profound as the difference between the sick and the well. Wilson was so sick that he
65 looked guilty, unforgivably guilty—as if he had just got some poor girl with child.

"I'll let you have that car," said Tom. "I'll send it over tomorrow afternoon."

---

8 **snort**: force air through the nostrils with a loud noise to show contempt, impatience, etc.   20 **stall**: (here) stop due to some malfunction   49 **flurry**: short sudden rush   52 **get wised up to sth.** (sl): become aware of sth.   57 **relentless**: constant   59 **alight on sb./sth.**: (here) land of fall on sb.

That locality was always vaguely disquieting, even in the broad glare of afternoon, and now I turned my head as though I had been warned of something behind. Over the ashheaps the giant eyes of Doctor T.-J.-Eckleburg kept their vigil but I perceived, after a moment, that other eyes were regarding us with peculiar intensity from less than 5 twenty feet away.

In one of the windows over the garage the curtains had been moved aside a little and Myrtle Wilson was peering down at the car. So engrossed was she that she had no consciousness of being observed and one emotion after another crept into her face like objects into a slowly 10 developing picture. Her expression was curiously familiar—it was an expression I had often seen on women's faces but on Myrtle Wilson's face it seemed purposeless and inexplicable until I realized that her eyes, wide with jealous terror, were fixed not on Tom but on Jordan Baker, whom she took to be his wife. 15

There is no confusion like the confusion of a simple mind and as we drove away Tom was feeling the hot whips of panic. His wife and his mistress, until an hour ago secure and inviolate, were slipping precipitately from his control. Instinct made him step on the accelerator with the double purpose of overtaking Daisy and leaving Wilson behind, and 20 we sped along toward Astoria at fifty miles an hour until, among the spidery girders of the elevated, we came in sight of the easygoing blue coupé.

"Those big movies around Fiftieth Street are cool," suggested Jordan. "I love New York on summer afternoons when everyone's away. There's 25 something very sensuous about it—overripe, as if all sorts of funny fruits were going to fall into your hands."

The word "sensuous" had the effect of further disquieting Tom, but before he could invent a protest the coupé came to a stop and Daisy signalled us to draw up alongside. 30

"Where are we going?" she cried.

"How about the movies?"

"It's so hot," she complained. "You go. We'll ride around and meet you after." With an effort her wit rose faintly, "We'll meet you on some corner. I'll be the man smoking two cigarettes." 35

"We can't argue about it here," Tom said impatiently, as a truck gave out a cursing whistle behind us. "You follow me to the south side of Central Park, in front of the Plaza."

Several times he turned his head and looked back for their car, and if the traffic delayed them he slowed up until they came into sight. I think he was afraid they would dart down a side street and out of his life forever.

But they didn't. And we all took the less explicable step of engaging the parlor of a suite in the Plaza Hotel.

The prolonged and tumultuous argument that ended by herding us into that room eludes me, though I have a sharp physical memory that, in the course of it, my underwear kept climbing like a damp snake around my legs and intermittent beads of sweat raced cool across my back. The notion originated with Daisy's suggestion that we hire five bathrooms and take cold baths, and then assumed more tangible form as "a place to have a mint julep." Each of us said over and over that it was a "crazy idea"—we all talked at once to a baffled clerk and thought, or pretended to think, that we were being very funny. . . .

The room was large and stifling, and, though it was already four o'clock, opening the windows admitted only a gust of hot shrubbery from the Park. Daisy went to the mirror and stood with her back to us fixing her hair.

"It's a swell suite," whispered Jordan respectfully and everyone laughed.

"Open another window," commanded Daisy, without turning around.

"There aren't any more."

"Well, we'd better telephone for an axe——"

"The thing to do is to forget about the heat," said Tom impatiently. "You make it ten times worse by crabbing about it."

1 **disquieting**: causing anxiety   18 **inviolate** (fml): that cannot be harmed
18–19 **precipitate** [prɪˈsɪpɪtət]: impulsive; violently hurried   22 **easygoing**: (here)
comfortable   41 **dart** (v): move suddenly and fast   44 **parlor** (old use): room
where one can receive visitors or talk privately   51 **mintjulep** (AE): drink made of
liquor and ice with fresh mint   52 **baffle sb.**: puzzle sb.   54 **stifling** [ˈstaɪflɪŋ]
(adj): oppressively hot   58 **swell** (AE infml): excellent   65 **crab about sth.** (infml,
derog): complain about sth.

He unrolled the bottle of whiskey from the towel and put it on the table.

"Why not let her alone, old sport," remarked Gatsby. "You're the one that wanted to come to town."

There was a moment of silence. The telephone book slipped from its 5 nail and splashed to the floor, whereupon Jordan whispered "Excuse me"—but this time no one laughed.

"I'll pick it up," I offered.

"I've got it." Gatsby examined the parted string, muttered "Hum!" in an interested way, and tossed the book on a chair. 10

"That's a great expression of yours, isn't it?" said Tom sharply.

"What is?"

"All this 'old sport' business. Where'd you pick that up?"

"Now see here, Tom," said Daisy, turning around from the mirror, "if you're going to make personal remarks I won't stay here a minute. Call 15 up and order some ice for the mint julep."

As Tom took up the receiver the compressed heat exploded into sound and we were listening to the portentous chords of Mendelssohn's Wedding March from the ballroom below.

"Imagine marrying anybody in this heat!" cried Jordan dismally. 20

"Still—I was married in the middle of June," Daisy remembered. "Louisville in June! Somebody fainted. Who was it fainted, Tom?"

"Biloxi," he answered shortly.

"A man named Biloxi. 'Blocks' Biloxi, and he made boxes—that's a fact—and he was from Biloxi, Tennessee." 25

"They carried him into my house," appended Jordan, "because we lived just two doors from the church. And he stayed three weeks, until Daddy told him he had to get out. The day after he left Daddy died." After a moment she added as if she might have sounded irreverent, "There wasn't any connection." 30

"I used to know a Bill Biloxi from Memphis," I remarked.

"That was his cousin. I knew his whole family history before he left. He gave me an aluminum putter that I use today."

The music had died down as the ceremony began and now a long cheer floated in at the window, followed by intermittent cries of "Yea— 35 ea—ea!" and finally by a burst of jazz as the dancing began.

"We're getting old," said Daisy. "If we were young we'd rise and dance."

"Remember Biloxi," Jordan warned her. "Where'd you know him, 40 Tom?"

"Biloxi?" He concentrated with an effort. "I didn't know him. He was a friend of Daisy's."

"He was not," she denied. "I'd never seen him before. He came down in the private car."

45 "Well, he said he knew you. He said he was raised in Louisville. Asa Bird brought him around at the last minute and asked if we had room for him."

Jordan smiled.

"He was probably bumming his way home. He told me he was 50 president of your class at Yale."

Tom and I looked at each other blankly.

"Biloxi?"

"First place we didn't have any president—"

Gatsby's foot beat a short restless tattoo and Tom eyed him 55 suddenly.

"By the way, Mr. Gatsby, I understand you're an Oxford man."

"Not exactly."

"Oh, yes, I understand you went to Oxford."

"Yes—I went there."

60 A pause. Then Tom's voice, incredulous and insulting:

"You must have gone there about the time Biloxi went to New Haven."

Another pause. A waiter knocked and came in with crushed mint and ice but the silence was unbroken by his "Thank you" and the soft 65 closing of the door. This tremendous detail was to be cleared up at last.

"I told you I went there," said Gatsby.

---

10 **toss sth.**: throw sth. slightly or carelessly   18 **portentous** (derog): pompously solemn   19 **Wedding March**: section of the concert overture "A Midsummer Night's Dream" by Felix Mendelsson-Bartholdy (1809–1847)   26 **append** (fml): add 29 **irreverent**: feeling or showing no respect for sacred things   33 **putter**: golf club used for putting (i.e. hitting the ball with a light stroke so that it rolls nearer to or into the hole)   49 **bum** (v): travel without purpose   54 **tattoo**: act of drumming and tapping

"I heard you, but I'd like to know when."

"It was in nineteen-nineteen. I only stayed five months. That's why I can't really call myself an Oxford man."

Tom glanced around to see if we mirrored his unbelief. But we were all looking at Gatsby. 5

"It was an opportunity they gave to some of the officers after the Armistice," he continued. "We could go to any of the universities in England or France."

I wanted to get up and slap him on the back. I had one of those renewals of complete faith in him that I'd experienced before. 10

Daisy rose, smiling faintly, and went to the table.

"Open the whiskey, Tom," she ordered. "And I'll make you a mint julep. Then you won't seem so stupid to yourself. . . . Look at the mint!"

"Wait a minute," snapped Tom. "I want to ask Mr. Gatsby one more 15 question."

"Go on," Gatsby said politely.

"What kind of a row are you trying to cause in my house anyhow?"

They were out in the open at last and Gatsby was content.

"He isn't causing a row." Daisy looked desperately from one to the 20 other. "You're causing a row. Please have a little self control."

"Self control!" repeated Tom incredulously. "I suppose the latest thing is to sit back and let Mr. Nobody from Nowhere make love to your wife. Well, if that's the idea you can count me out. . . . Nowadays people begin by sneering at family life and family institutions and next they'll throw 25 everything overboard and have intermarriage between black and white."

Flushed with his impassioned gibberish he saw himself standing alone on the last barrier of civilization.

"We're all white here," murmured Jordan. 30

"I know I'm not very popular. I don't give big parties. I suppose you've got to make your house into a pigsty in order to have any friends—in the modern world."

Angry as I was, as we all were, I was tempted to laugh whenever he opened his mouth. The transition from libertine to prig was so 35 complete.

"I've got something to tell *you*, old sport,—" began Gatsby. But Daisy guessed at his intention.

"Please don't!" she interrupted helplessly. "Please let's all go home.
40 Why don't we all go home?"

"That's a good idea." I got up. "Come on, Tom. Nobody wants a drink."

"I want to know what Mr. Gatsby has to tell me."

"Your wife doesn't love you," said Gatsby quietly. "She's never loved
45 you. She loves me."

"You must be crazy!" exclaimed Tom automatically.

Gatsby sprang to his feet, vivid with excitement.

"She never loved you, do you hear?" he cried. "She only married you because I was poor and she was tired of waiting for me. It was a terrible
50 mistake, but in her heart she never loved anyone except me!"

At this point Jordan and I tried to go but Tom and Gatsby insisted with competitive firmness that we remain—as though neither of them had anything to conceal and it would be a privilege to partake vicariously of their emotions.

55 "Sit down, Daisy." Tom's voice groped unsuccessfully for the paternal note. "What's been going on? I want to hear all about it."

"I told you what's been going on," said Gatsby. "Going on for five years—and you didn't know."

Tom turned to Daisy sharply.

60 "You've been seeing this fellow for five years?"

"Not seeing," said Gatsby. "No, we couldn't meet. But both of us loved each other all that time, old sport, and you didn't know. I used to laugh sometimes—" but there was no laughter in his eyes, "to think that you didn't know."

65 "Oh—that's all." Tom tapped his thick fingers together like a clergyman and leaned back in his chair.

---

18 **row** [raʊ]: loud quarrel   25 **sneer at sb./sth.**: express contempt of sb./sth.
28 **flushed with sth.**: very excited by sth.   **gibberish** ['dʒɪbərɪʃ]: nonsense
35 **libertine**: man who lives an irresponsible and immoral life   **prig** (infml, derog):
person who behaves as if he or she were morally superior to others, and who
disapproves of what others do   53 **partake of sth.** (fml): have some of the qualities
of sth.; (rare) take a part in sth.   **vicarious**: experienced indirectly; experienced by
one person on behalf of another   55 **grope for sth.**: search for sth.

"You're crazy!" he exploded. "I can't speak about what happened five years ago because I didn't know Daisy then—and I'll be damned if I see how you got within a mile of her unless you brought the groceries to the back door. But all the rest of that's a God Damned lie. Daisy loved me when she married me and she loves me now." 5

"No," said Gatsby, shaking his head.

"She does, though. The trouble is that sometimes she gets foolish ideas in her head and doesn't know what she's doing." He nodded sagely. "And what's more, I love Daisy too. Once in a while I go off on a spree and make a fool of myself, but I always come back, and in my heart I 10 love her all the time."

"You're revolting," said Daisy. She turned to me and her voice, dropping an octave lower, filled the room with thrilling scorn: "Do you know why we left Chicago? I'm surprised that they didn't treat you to the story of that little spree." 15

Gatsby walked over and stood beside her.

"Daisy, that's all over now," he said earnestly. "It doesn't matter any more. Just tell him the truth—that you never loved him—and it's all wiped out forever."

She looked at him blindly. "Why,—how could I love him—pos- 20 sibly?"

"You never loved him."

She hesitated. Her eyes fell on Jordan and me with a sort of appeal, as though she realized at last what she was doing—and as though she had never, all along, intended doing anything at all. But it was done 25 now. It was too late.

"I never loved him," she said, with perceptible reluctance.

"Not at Kapiolani?" demanded Tom suddenly.

"No."

From the ballroom beneath, muffled and suffocating chords were 30 drifting up on hot waves of air.

"Not that day I carried you down from the Punch Bowl to keep your shoes dry?" There was a husky tenderness in his tone. "… Daisy?"

"Please don't." Her voice was cold but the rancour was gone from it. She looked at Gatsby. "There, Jay," she said—but her hand as she tried 35 to light a cigarette was trembling. Suddenly she threw the cigarette and the burning match on the carpet.

"Oh, you want too much!" she cried to Gatsby. "I love you now—isn't that enough? I can't help what's past." She began to sob helplessly. "I did
40 love him once—but I loved you too."

Gatsby's eyes opened and closed.

"You loved me *too*?" he repeated.

"Even that's a lie," said Tom savagely. "She didn't know you were alive. Why,—there're things between Daisy and me that you'll never
45 know, things that neither of us can ever forget."

The words seemed to bite physically into Gatsby.

"I want to speak to Daisy alone," he insisted. "She's all excited now——"

"Even alone I can't say I never loved Tom," she admitted in a pitiful
50 voice. "It wouldn't be true."

"Of course it wouldn't," agreed Tom.

She turned to her husband.

"As if it mattered to you," she said.

"Of course it matters. I'm going to take better care of you from now
55 on."

"You don't understand," said Gatsby, with a touch of panic. "You're not going to take care of her any more."

"I'm not?" Tom opened his eyes wide and laughed. He could afford to control himself now. "Why's that?"

60 "Daisy's leaving you."

"Nonsense."

"I am, though," she said with a visible effort.

"She's not leaving me!" Tom's words suddenly leaned down over Gatsby. "Certainly not for a common swindler who'd have to steal the
65 ring he put on her finger."

"I won't stand this!" cried Daisy. "Oh, please let's get out."

"Who are you anyhow?" broke out Tom. "You're one of that bunch that hangs around with Meyer Wolfshiem—that much I happen to

8 **sage** (fml): wise or wise-looking   9 **spree** (infml): period of wild, irresponsible fun   14 **treat sb. to sth.**: give sb. sth. enjoyable to hear   28 **Kapiolani**: park on the Hawaiian island of Oahu, Hawaii   30 **muffle**: (of sounds) heard vaguely because an obstacle is in the way   **suffocate sth.**: suppress sth.   32 **Punch Bowl**: peak on the island of Oahu, Hawaii   34 **rancour** ['ræŋkər]: deep long-lasting bitterness

know. I've made a little investigation into your affairs—and I'll carry it further tomorrow."

"You can suit yourself about that, old sport," said Gatsby steadily.

"I found out what your 'drug stores' were." He turned to us and spoke rapidly. "He and this Wolfshiem bought up a lot of side-street 5 drug stores here and in Chicago and sold grain alcohol over the counter. That's one of his little stunts. I picked him for a bootlegger the first time I saw him and I wasn't far wrong."

"What about it?" said Gatsby politely. "I guess your friend Walter Chase wasn't too proud to come in on it." 10

"And you left him in the lurch, didn't you? You let him go to jail for a month over in New Jersey. God! You ought to hear Walter on the subject of *you*."

"He came to us dead broke. He was very glad to pick up some money, old sport." 15

"Don't you call me 'old sport'!" cried Tom. Gatsby said nothing. "Walter could have you up on the betting laws too, but Wolfshiem scared him into shutting his mouth."

That unfamiliar yet recognizable look was back again in Gatsby's face. 20

"That drug store business was just small change," continued Tom slowly, "but you've got something on now that Walter's afraid to tell me about."

I glanced at Daisy who was staring terrified between Gatsby and her husband and at Jordan who had begun to balance an invisible but 25 absorbing object on the tip of her chin. Then I turned back to Gatsby— and was startled at his expression. He looked—and this is said in all contempt for the babbled slander of his garden—as if he had "killed a man." For a moment the set of his face could be described in just that fantastic way. 30

It passed, and he began to talk excitedly to Daisy, denying everything, defending his name against accusations that had not been made. But with every word she was drawing further and further into herself, so he gave that up and only the dead dream fought on as the afternoon slipped away, trying to touch what was no longer tangible, struggling unhappily, 35 undespairingly, toward that lost voice across the room.

The voice begged again to go.

"*Please,* Tom! I can't stand this any more."

Her frightened eyes told that whatever intentions, whatever courage
40 she had had, were definitely gone.

"You two start on home, Daisy," said Tom. "In Mr. Gatsby's car."

She looked at Tom, alarmed now, but he insisted with magnanimous
scorn.

"Go on. He won't annoy you. I think he realizes that his presumptuous
45 little flirtation is over."

They were gone, without a word, snapped out, made accidental,
isolated like ghosts even from our pity.

After a moment Tom got up and began wrapping the unopened
bottle of whiskey in the towel.

50 "Want any of this stuff? Jordan? … Nick?"

I didn't answer.

"Nick?" He asked again.

"What?"

"Want any?"

55 "No … I just remembered that today's my birthday."

I was thirty. Before me stretched the portentous menacing road of a
new decade.

It was seven o'clock when we got into the coupé with him and started
for Long Island. Tom talked incessantly, exulting and laughing, but his
60 voice was as remote from Jordan and me as the foreign clamor on the
sidewalk or the tumult of the elevated overhead. Human sympathy has
its limits and we were content to let all their tragic arguments fade with
the city lights behind. Thirty—the promise of a decade of loneliness, a
thinning list of single men to know, a thinning brief-case of enthusiasm,
65 thinning hair. But there was Jordan beside me who, unlike Daisy, was
too wise ever to carry well-forgotten dreams from age to age. As we

11 **leave sb. in the lurch**: leave sb. in a difficult situation   14 **dead broke** (infml):
absolutely penniless   17 **have sb. up on sth.** (infml): cause sb. to be accused of sth.
(esp. a crime)   21 **small change**: (here) unimportant source of income   28 **babble**:
chatter in a thoughtless or confused way   **slander**: false statement to damage sb.'s
reputation   36 **undespairing**: ever-hoping   42 **magnanimous** [mægˈnænɪməs]: of a
generous frame of mind   43 **scorn**: strong contempt   44 **presumptuous**: showing
arrogance   56 **portentous**: of great importance   **menace sb./sth.**: threaten sb.
60 **clamor**: loud, confused noise

passed over the dark bridge, her wan face fell lazily against my coat's shoulder and the formidable stroke of thirty died away with the reassuring pressure of her hand.

So we drove on toward death through the cooling twilight.

The young Greek, Michaelis, who ran the coffee joint beside the ashheaps, was the principal witness at the inquest. He had slept through the heat, until after five, when he strolled over to the garage and found George Wilson sick in his office—really sick, pale as his own pale hair and shaking all over. Michaelis advised him to go to bed but Wilson refused, saying that he'd miss a lot of business if he did. While his neighbor was trying to persuade him a violent racket broke out overhead.

"I've got my wife locked in up there," explained Wilson calmly. "She's going to stay there till the day after tomorrow and then we're going to move away."

Michaelis was astonished; they had been neighbors for four years and Wilson had never seemed faintly capable of such a statement. Generally he was one of these worn-out men: when he wasn't working he sat on a chair in the doorway and stared at the people and the cars that passed along the road. When anyone spoke to him he invariably laughed in an agreeable colorless way. He was his wife's man and not his own.

So naturally Michaelis tried to find out what had happened, but Wilson wouldn't say a word—instead he began to throw curious, suspicious glances at his visitor and ask him what he'd been doing at certain times on certain days. Just as the latter was getting uneasy, some workmen came past the door bound for his restaurant and Michaelis took the opportunity to get away, intending to come back later. But he didn't. He supposed he forgot to, that's all. When he came outside again a little after seven he was reminded of the conversation because he heard Mrs. Wilson's voice, loud and scolding, downstairs in the garage.

"Beat me!" he heard her cry. "Throw me down and beat me, you dirty little coward!"

A moment later she rushed out into the dusk, waving her hands and shouting; before he could move from his door the business was over.

The "death car," as the newspapers called it, didn't stop; it came out of the gathering darkness, wavered tragically for a moment and then

disappeared around the next bend. Michaelis wasn't even sure of its color—he told the first policeman that it was light green. The other car, the one going toward New York, came to rest a hundred yards beyond,
40   and its driver hurried back to where Myrtle Wilson, her life violently extinguished, knelt in the road and mingled her thick, dark blood with the dust.

Michaelis and this man reached her first, but when they had torn open her shirtwaist still damp with perspiration, they saw that her left
45   breast was swinging loose like a flap and there was no need to listen for the heart beneath. The mouth was wide open and ripped at the corners as though she had choked a little in giving up the tremendous vitality she had stored so long.

We saw the three or four automobiles and the crowd when we were still
50   some distance away.

"Wreck!" said Tom. "That's good. Wilson'll have a little business at last."

He slowed down, but still without any intention of stopping until, as we came nearer, the hushed intent faces of the people at the garage door
55   made him automatically put on the brakes.

"We'll take a look," he said doubtfully, "just a look."

I became aware now of a hollow, wailing sound which issued incessantly from the garage, a sound which as we got out of the coupé and walked toward the door resolved itself into the words "Oh My God!"
60   uttered over and over in a gasping moan.

"There's some bad trouble here," said Tom excitedly.

He reached up on tiptoes and peered over a circle of heads into the garage which was lit only by a yellow light in a swinging wire basket overhead. Then he made a harsh sound in his throat and with a violent,
65   thrusting movement of his powerful arms pushed his way through.

The circle closed up again with a running murmur of expostulation; it was a minute before I could see anything at all. Then new arrivals disarranged the line and Jordan and I were pushed suddenly inside.

6 **inquest**: official inquiry to discover the facts about a violent or suspicious death
36 **gather**: (here) increase   **waver**: move unsteadily   45 **flap**: flat piece of material that covers an opening or hangs down   54 **intent** (adj): full of eager interest
60 **moan**: long mournful sound   66 **expostulation**: protest

Myrtle Wilson's body wrapped in a blanket and then in another blanket as though she suffered from a chill in the hot night lay on a work table by the wall and Tom, with his back to us, was bending over it, motionless. Next to him stood a motor cycle policeman taking down names with much sweat and correction in a little book. At first I couldn't 5 find the source of the high, groaning words that echoed clamorously through the bare garage—then I saw Wilson standing on the raised threshold of his office, swaying back and forth and holding to the doorposts with both hands. Some man was talking to him in a low voice and attempting from time to time to lay a hand on his shoulder, but 10 Wilson neither heard nor saw. His eyes would drop slowly from the swinging light to the laden table by the wall and then jerk back to the light again and he gave out incessantly his high horrible call.

"O my Ga-od! O my Ga-od! O Ga-od! O my Ga-od!"

Presently Tom lifted his head with a jerk and after staring around the 15 garage with glazed eyes addressed a mumbled incoherent remark to the policeman.

"M-a-v—" the policeman was saying, "—o—"

"No, —r—" corrected the man, "M-a-v-r-o——"

"Listen to me!" muttered Tom fiercely. 20

"r—" said the policeman, "o——"

"g——"

"g—" He looked up as Tom's broad hand fell sharply on his shoulder. "What you want, fella?"

"What happened—that's what I want to know!" 25

"Auto hit her. Ins'antly killed."

"Instantly killed," repeated Tom, staring.

"She ran out ina road. Son-of-a-bitch didn't even stopus car."

"There was two cars," said Michaelis. "One comin', one goin', see?"

"Going where?" asked the policeman keenly. 30

"One goin' each way. Well, she—" His hand rose toward the blankets but stopped half way and fell to his side, "—she ran out there an' the one comin' from N'York knock right into her goin' thirty or forty miles an hour."

"What's the name of this place here?" demanded the officer. 35

"Hasn't got any name."

A pale, well dressed Negro stepped near.

"It was a yellow car," he said. "Big yellow car. New."

"See the accident?" asked the policeman.

40 "No, but the car passed me down the road, going faster'n forty. Going fifty, sixty."

"Come here and let's have your name. Look out now. I want to get his name."

Some words of this conversation must have reached Wilson swaying
45 in the office door for suddenly a new theme found voice among his gasping cries.

"You don't have to tell me what kind of car it was! I know what kind of car it was!"

Watching Tom I saw the wad of muscle back of his shoulder tighten
50 under his coat. He walked quickly over to Wilson and standing in front of him seized him firmly by the upper arms.

"You've got to pull yourself together," he said with soothing gruffness.

Wilson's eyes fell upon Tom; he started up on his tiptoes and then
55 would have collapsed to his knees had not Tom held him upright.

"Listen," said Tom, shaking him a little. "I just got here a minute ago, from New York. I was bringing you that coupé we've been talking about. That yellow car I was driving this afternoon wasn't mine, do you hear? I haven't seen it all afternoon."

60 Only the Negro and I were near enough to hear what he said but the policeman caught something in the tone and looked over with truculent eyes.

"What's all that?" he demanded.

"I'm a friend of his." Tom turned his head but kept his hands firm on
65 Wilson's body. "He says he knows the car that did it. . . . It was a yellow car."

Some dim impulse moved the policeman to look suspiciously at Tom.

---

16 **mumble**: speak unclearly and quietly   26 **ins'antly** (non-standard pron):
instantly   28 **stopus** (non-standard pron): stop his   40 **faster'n** (non-standard
pron): faster than   46 **gasp**: take quick deep breaths with open mouth   49 **wad**
(sl): large amount   52 **soothing**: comforting   53 **gruffness**: (of a voice)
roughness   61 **truculent** ['trʌkjələnt] (derog): defiant and aggressive

"And what color's your car?"

"It's a blue car, a coupé."

"We've come straight from New York," I said.

Someone who had been driving a little behind us confirmed this and the policeman turned away.

"Now if you'll let me have that name again correct——"

Picking up Wilson like a doll, Tom carried him into the office, set him down in a chair and came back.

"If somebody'll come here and sit with him!" he snapped authoritatively. He watched while the two men standing closest glanced at each other and went unwillingly into the room. Then Tom shut the door on them and came down the single step, his eyes avoiding the table. As he passed close to me he whispered "Let's get out."

Self-consciously, with his authoritative arms breaking the way, we pushed through the still gathering crowd, passing a hurried doctor, case in hand, who had been sent for in wild hope half an hour ago.

Tom drove slowly until we were beyond the bend—then his foot came down hard and the coupé raced along through the night. In a little while I heard a low husky sob and saw that the tears were overflowing down his face.

"The God Damn coward!" he whimpered. "He didn't even stop his car."

The Buchanans' house floated suddenly toward us through the dark, rustling trees. Tom stopped beside the porch and looked up at the second floor where two windows bloomed with light among the vines.

"Daisy's home," he said. As we got out of the car he glanced at me and frowned slightly.

"I ought to have dropped you in West Egg, Nick. There's nothing we can do tonight."

A change had come over him and he spoke gravely, and with decision. As we walked across the moonlit gravel to the porch he disposed of the situation in a few brisk phrases.

"I'll telephone for a taxi to take you home, and while you're waiting, you and Jordan better go in the kitchen and have them get you some supper—if you want any." He opened the door. "Come in."

"No thanks. But I'd be glad if you'd order me the taxi. I'll wait outside."

Jordan put her hand on my arm.

"Won't you come in, Nick?"

40 "No, thanks."

I was feeling a little sick and I wanted to be alone. But Jordan lingered for a moment more.

"It's only half past nine," she said.

I'd be damned if I'd go in; I'd had enough of all of them for one day, 45 and suddenly that included Jordan too. She must have seen something of this in my expression for she turned abruptly away and ran up the porch steps into the house. I sat down for a few minutes with my head in my hands, until I heard the phone taken up inside and the butler's voice calling a taxi. Then I walked slowly down the drive away from the 50 house, intending to wait by the gate.

I hadn't gone twenty yards when I heard my name and Gatsby stepped from between two bushes into the path. I must have felt pretty weird by that time because I could think of nothing except the luminosity of his pink suit under the moon.

55 "What are you doing?" I inquired.

"Just standing here, old sport."

Somehow that seemed a despicable occupation. For all I knew he was going to rob the house in a moment; I wouldn't have been surprised to see sinister faces, the faces of "Wolfshiem's people," behind him in the 60 dark shrubbery.

"Did you see any trouble on the road?" he asked after a minute.

"Yes."

He hesitated.

"Was she killed?"

65 "Yes."

"I thought so; I told Daisy I thought so. It's better that the shock should all come at once. She stood it pretty well."

---

24 **rustle**: make a dry light sound 31 **dispose of sb./sth.**: finish with sb./sth. that presents a problem 32 **brisk**: quick; energetic 52 **weird**: strange
53 **luminosity**: quality of being full of light 57 **despicable**: deserving to be despised

He spoke as if Daisy's reaction was the only thing that mattered.

"I got to West Egg by a side road," he went on, "and left the car in my garage. I don't think anybody saw us but of course I can't be sure."

I disliked him so much by this time that I didn't find it necessary to tell him he was wrong. 5

"Who was the woman?" he inquired.

"Her name was Wilson. Her husband owns the garage. How the devil did it happen?"

"Well, I tried to swing the wheel——" He broke off, and suddenly I guessed at the truth. 10

"Was Daisy driving?"

"Yes," he said after a moment, "but of course I'll say I was. You see, when we left New York she was very nervous and she thought it would steady her to drive—and this woman rushed out at us just as we were passing a car coming the other way. It all happened in a minute but it 15 seemed to me that she wanted to speak to us, thought we were somebody she knew. Well, first Daisy turned away from the woman toward the other car, and then she lost her nerve and turned back. The second my hand reached the wheel I felt the shock—it must have killed her instantly." 20

"It ripped her open——"

"Don't tell me, old sport." He winced. "Anyhow—Daisy stepped on it. I tried to make her stop, but she couldn't so I pulled on the emergency brake. Then she fell over into my lap and I drove on.

"She'll be all right tomorrow," he said presently. "I'm just going to 25 wait here and see if he tries to bother her about that unpleasantness this afternoon. She's locked herself into her room and if he tries any brutality she's going to turn the light out and on again."

"He won't touch her," I said. "He's not thinking about her."

"I don't trust him, old sport." 30

"How long are you going to wait?"

"All night if necessary. Anyhow till they all go to bed."

A new point of view occurred to me. Suppose Tom found out that Daisy had been driving. He might think he saw a connection in it—he might think anything. I looked at the house: there were two or three 35 bright windows downstairs and the pink glow from Daisy's room on the second floor.

"You wait here," I said. "I'll see if there's any sign of a commotion."

I walked back along the border of the lawn, traversed the gravel
40 softly and tiptoed up the veranda steps. The drawing room curtains
were open and I saw that the room was empty. Crossing the porch where
we had dined that June night three months before, I came to a small
rectangle of light which I guessed was the pantry window. The blind
was drawn but I found a rift at the sill.

45 Daisy and Tom were sitting opposite each other at the kitchen table
with a plate of cold fried chicken between them and two bottles of ale.
He was talking intently across the table at her and in his earnestness his
hand had fallen upon and covered her own. Once in a while she looked
up at him and nodded in agreement.

50 They weren't happy, and neither of them had touched the chicken or
the ale—and yet they weren't unhappy either. There was an unmistakable
air of natural intimacy about the picture and anybody would have said
that they were conspiring together.

As I tiptoed from the porch I heard my taxi feeling its way along the
55 dark road toward the house. Gatsby was waiting where I had left him in
the drive.

"Is it all quiet up there?" he asked anxiously.

"Yes, it's all quiet." I hesitated. "You'd better come home and get some
sleep."

60 He shook his head.

"I want to wait here till Daisy goes to bed. Good night, old sport."

He put his hands in his coat pockets and turned back eagerly to his
scrutiny of the house, as though my presence marred the sacredness of
the vigil. So I walked away and left him standing there in the moonlight—
65 watching over nothing.

14 **steady sb.**: calm sb. down   22 **wince**: show pain or distress by a slight
movement of the muscles in one's face   44 **rift**: opening   **sill**: base of a window
63 **scrutiny**: careful and thorough examination   **mar sth.**: damage sth.
sacredness: quality of being solemn or holy

Chapter 8

I couldn't sleep all night; a fog-horn was groaning incessantly on the Sound, and I tossed half sick between grotesque reality and savage frightening dreams. Toward dawn I heard a taxi go up Gatsby's drive and immediately I jumped out of bed and began to dress—I felt that I had something to tell him, something to warn him about and morning 5 would be too late.

Crossing his lawn I saw that his front door was still open and he was leaning against a table in the hall, heavy with dejection or sleep.

"Nothing happened," he said wanly. "I waited, and about four o'clock she came to the window and stood there for a minute and then turned 10 out the light."

His house had never seemed so enormous to me as it did that night when we hunted through the great rooms for cigarettes. We pushed aside curtains that were like pavilions and felt over innumerable feet of dark wall for electric light switches—once I tumbled with a sort of 15 splash upon the keys of a ghostly piano. There was an inexplicable amount of dust everywhere and the rooms were musty as though they hadn't been aired for many days. I found the humidor on an unfamiliar table with two stale dry cigarettes inside. Throwing open the French windows of the drawing room, we sat smoking out into the darkness. 20 "You ought to go away," I said. "It's pretty certain they'll trace your car."

"Go away *now*, old sport?"

"Go to Atlantic City for a week, or up to Montreal."

He wouldn't consider it. He couldn't possibly leave Daisy until he knew what she was going to do. He was clutching at some last hope and 25 I couldn't bear to shake him free.

It was this night that he told me the strange story of his youth with Dan Cody—told it to me because "Jay Gatsby" had broken up like glass against Tom's hard malice and the long secret extravaganza was played

30 out. I think that he would have acknowledged anything, now, without reserve, but he wanted to talk about Daisy.

She was the first "nice" girl he had ever known. In various unrevealed capacities he had come in contact with such people but always with indiscernible barbed wire between. He found her excitingly desirable.
35 He went to her house, at first with other officers from Camp Taylor, then alone. It amazed him—he had never been in such a beautiful house before. But what gave it an air of breathless intensity was that Daisy lived there—it was as casual a thing to her as his tent out at camp was to him. There was a ripe mystery about it, a hint of bedrooms upstairs
40 more beautiful and cool than other bedrooms, of gay and radiant activities taking place through its corridors and of romances that were not musty and laid away already in lavender, but fresh and breathing and redolent of this year's shining motor cars and of dances whose flowers were scarcely withered. It excited him too that many men had
45 already loved Daisy—it increased her value in his eyes. He felt their presence all about the house, pervading the air with the shades and echoes of still vibrant emotions.

But he knew that he was in Daisy's house by a colossal accident. However glorious might be his future as Jay Gatsby, he was at present a
50 penniless young man without a past, and at any moment the invisible cloak of his uniform might slip from his shoulders. So he made the most of his time. He took what he could get, ravenously and unscrupulously— eventually he took Daisy one still October night, took her because he had no real right to touch her hand.

55 He might have despised himself, for he had certainly taken her under false pretenses. I don't mean that he had traded on his phantom millions, but he had deliberately given Daisy a sense of security; he let her believe

---

8 **dejection**: depression   16 **splash** (n): *Platschen*   18 **humidor**: tobacco case equipped with a moistened sponge for keeping the air moist   19 **stale**: no longer fresh   23 **Atlantic City**: seaside resort in New Jersey   25 **clutch at sth.**: try to seize sth.   26 **shake sb. free**: (here) help sb. realize that sth. is over   29 **malice**: desire to harm others   **extravaganza**: (here) fantasy   32 **unrevealed** (adj): not made known   33 **capacity**: function   34 **indiscernible**: that cannot be understood 38 **casual**: (here) easy, obvious   39 **hint**: indication   42 **musty**: no longer smelling fresh   **lay sth. away**: (here) put sth. out of sight   43 **redolent of sth.** (fml): (here) strongly suggestive or reminiscent of sth.   44 **wither**: become dry or dead   52 **ravenous**: very hungry

that he was a person from much the same strata as herself—that he was
fully able to take care of her. As a matter of fact he had no such
facilities—he had no comfortable family standing behind him and he
was liable at the whim of an impersonal government to be blown
anywhere about the world.   5

But he didn't despise himself and it didn't turn out as he had
imagined. He had intended, probably, to take what he could and go—
but now he found that he had committed himself to the following of a
grail. He knew that Daisy was extraordinary, but he didn't realize just
how extraordinary a "nice" girl could be. She vanished into her rich   10
house, into her rich, full life, leaving Gatsby—nothing. He felt married
to her, that was all.

When they met again two days later it was Gatsby who was breathless,
who was somehow betrayed. Her porch was bright with the bought
luxury of star-shine; the wicker of the settee squeaked fashionably as she   15
turned toward him and he kissed her curious and lovely mouth. She
had caught a cold and it made her voice huskier and more charming
than ever and Gatsby was overwhelmingly aware of the youth and
mystery that wealth imprisons and preserves, of the freshness of many
clothes and of Daisy, gleaming like silver, safe and proud above the hot   20
struggles of the poor.

"I can't describe to you how surprised I was to find out I loved her, old
sport. I even hoped for a while that she'd throw me over, but she didn't,
because she was in love with me too. She thought I knew a lot because I
knew different things from her. . . . Well, there I was, way off my   25
ambitions, getting deeper in love every minute, and all of a sudden I
didn't care. What was the use of doing great things if I could have a
better time telling her what I was going to do?"

On the last afternoon before he went abroad, he sat with Daisy in his
arms for a long, silent time. It was a cold fall day with fire in the room   30
and her cheeks flushed. Now and then she moved and he changed his
arm a little and once he kissed her dark shining hair. The afternoon had
made them tranquil for a while as if to give them a deep memory for the
long parting the next day promised. They had never been closer in their
month of love nor communicated more profoundly one with another,   35

than when she brushed silent lips against his coat's shoulder or when he touched the end of her fingers, gently, as though she were asleep.

He did extraordinarily well in the war. He was a captain before he went to the front and following the Argonne battles he got his majority and
40 the command of the divisional machine guns. After the Armistice he tried frantically to get home but some complication or misunderstanding sent him to Oxford instead. He was worried now—there was a quality of nervous despair in Daisy's letters. She didn't see why he couldn't come. She was feeling the pressure of the world outside and she wanted
45 to see him and feel his presence beside her and be reassured that she was doing the right thing after all.

For Daisy was young and her artificial world was redolent of orchids and pleasant, cheerful snobbery and orchestras which set the rhythm of the year, summing up the sadness and suggestiveness of life in new
50 tunes. All night the saxophones wailed the hopeless comment of the "Beale Street Blues" while a hundred pairs of golden and silver slippers shuffled the shining dust. At the grey tea hour there were always rooms that throbbed incessantly with this low sweet fever, while fresh faces drifted here and there like rose petals blown by the sad horns around
55 the floor.

Through this twilight universe Daisy began to move again with the season; suddenly she was again keeping half a dozen dates a day with half a dozen men and drowsing asleep at dawn with the beads and chiffon of an evening dress tangled among dying orchids on the floor
60 beside her bed. And all the time something within her was crying for a decision. She wanted her life shaped now, immediately—and the

---

1 **stratum** (pl **strata**): social class   4 **liable** ['laɪəbl]: likely   **whim**: sudden desire or idea   9 **grail**: the chalice or cup from which Jesus drank at the Last Supper; in Christian mythology, the grail became the object of a search, since the person who found it would be saved; (here) intense quest   23 **throw sb. over**: abandon sb. 36 **brush sth. against sb./sth. else**: touch sb./sth. lightly with sth. else 39 **majority**: military rank of a major   41 **frantic**: hurried and excited, but disorganized   49 **suggestiveness**: quality of suggesting or conveying a certain atmosphere or feeling   51 **"Beale Street Blues"**: song written by W.C. Handy (1873–1958)   58 **drowse**: be half asleep

decision must be made by some force—of love, of money, of unquestionable practicality—that was close at hand.

That force took shape in the middle of spring with the arrival of Tom Buchanan. There was a wholesome bulkiness about his person and his position and Daisy was flattered. Doubtless there was a certain struggle   5
and a certain relief. The letter reached Gatsby while he was still at Oxford.

It was dawn now on Long Island and we went about opening the rest of the windows downstairs, filling the house with grey-turning, gold-turning light. The shadow of a tree fell abruptly across the dew and   10
ghostly birds began to sing among the blue leaves. There was a slow, pleasant movement in the air, scarcely a wind, promising a cool lovely day.

"I don't think she ever loved him." Gatsby turned around from a window and looked at me challengingly. "You must remember, old   15
sport, she was very excited this afternoon. He told her those things in a way that frightened her—that made it look as if I was some kind of cheap sharper. And the result was she hardly knew what she was saying."

He sat down gloomily.   20

"Of course she might have loved him, just for a minute, when they were first married—and loved me more even then, do you see?"

Suddenly he came out with a curious remark:

"In any case," he said, "it was just personal."

What could you make of that, except to suspect some intensity in his   25
conception of the affair that couldn't be measured?

He came back from France when Tom and Daisy were still on their wedding trip, and made a miserable but irresistible journey to Louisville on the last of his army pay. He stayed there a week, walking the streets where their footsteps had clicked together through the November night   30
and revisiting the out-of-the-way places to which they had driven in her white car. Just as Daisy's house had always seemed to him more mysterious and gay than other houses, so his idea of the city itself, even though she was gone from it, was pervaded with a melancholy beauty.

35   He left feeling that if he had searched harder he might have found
her—that he was leaving her behind. The day-coach—he was penniless
now—was hot. He went out to the open vestibule and sat down on a
folding chair, and the station slid away and the backs of unfamiliar
buildings moved by. Then out into the spring fields, where a yellow
40   trolley raced them for a minute with people in it who might once have
seen the pale magic of her face along the casual street.

The track curved and now it was going away from the sun which, as
it sank lower, seemed to spread itself in benediction over the vanishing
city where she had drawn her breath. He stretched out his hand
45   desperately as if to snatch only a wisp of air, to save a fragment of the
spot that she had made lovely for him. But it was all going by too fast
now for his blurred eyes and he knew that he had lost that part of it, the
freshest and the best, forever.

It was nine o'clock when we finished breakfast and went out on the
50   porch. The night had made a sharp difference in the weather and there
was an autumn flavor in the air. The gardener, the last one of Gatsby's
former servants, came to the foot of the steps.

"I'm going to drain the pool today, Mr. Gatsby. Leaves'll start falling
pretty soon and then there's always trouble with the pipes."

55   "Don't do it today," Gatsby answered. He turned to me apologetically.
"You know, old sport, I've never used that pool all summer?"

I looked at my watch and stood up.

"Twelve minutes to my train."

I didn't want to go to the city. I wasn't worth a decent stroke of work
60   but it was more than that—I didn't want to leave Gatsby. I missed that
train, and then another, before I could get myself away.

"I'll call you up," I said finally.

"Do, old sport."

---

4 **bulkiness**: quality of being big and strong   18 **sharper** (AE sl): swindler, esp. one
who makes a living by cheating at cards   36 **day-coach** (AE): train carriage in
which one can sit but not lie down during the night   37 **vestibule** (AE): enclosed
space between passenger coaches on a train   40 **trolley**: low cart or truck
43 **benediction**: blessing   55 **apologetic**: feeling or expressing regret
59 **stroke** (n): successful action

"I'll call you about noon."

We walked slowly down the steps.

"I suppose Daisy'll call too." He looked at me anxiously as if he hoped I'd corroborate this.

"I suppose so."   5

"Well—goodbye."

We shook hands and I started away. Just before I reached the hedge I remembered something and turned around.

"They're a rotten crowd," I shouted, across the lawn. "You're worth the whole damn bunch put together."   10

I've always been glad I said that. It was the only compliment I ever gave him, because I disapproved of him from beginning to end. First he nodded politely, and then his face broke into that radiant and under-standing smile, as if we'd been in ecstatic cahoots on that fact all the time. His gorgeous pink rag of a suit made a bright spot of color against   15 the white steps and I thought of the night when I first came to his ancestral home three months before. The lawn and drive had been crowded with the faces of those who guessed at his corruption—and he had stood on those steps, concealing his incorruptible dream, as he waved them goodbye.   20

I thanked him for his hospitality. We were always thanking him for that—I and the others.

"Goodbye," I called. "I enjoyed breakfast, Gatsby."

Up in the city I tried for a while to list the quotations on an interminable amount of stock, then I fell asleep in my swivel chair. Just before noon   25 the phone woke me and I started up with sweat breaking out on my forehead. It was Jordan Baker; she often called me up at this hour because the uncertainty of her own movements between hotels and clubs and private houses made her hard to find in any other way. Usually her voice came over the wire as something fresh and cool as if a divot   30 from a green golf links had come sailing in at the office window but this morning it seemed harsh and dry.

"I've left Daisy's house," she said. "I'm at Hempstead and I'm going down to Southampton this afternoon."

Probably it had been tactful to leave Daisy's house, but the act   35 annoyed me and her next remark made me rigid.

"You weren't so nice to me last night."

"How could it have mattered then?"

Silence for a moment. Then—

40 "However—I want to see you."

"I want to see you too."

"Suppose I don't go to Southampton, and come into town this afternoon?"

"No—I don't think this afternoon."

45 "Very well."

"It's impossible this afternoon. Various——"

We talked like that for a while and then abruptly we weren't talking any longer. I don't know which of us hung up with a sharp click, but I know I didn't care. I couldn't have talked to her across a teatable that

50 day if I never talked to her again in this world.

I called Gatsby's house a few minutes later, but the line was busy. I tried four times; finally an exasperated central told me the wire was being kept open for long distance from Detroit. Taking out my time-table I drew a small circle around the three-fifty train. Then I leaned

55 back in my chair and tried to think. It was just noon.

When I passed the ashheaps on the train that morning I had crossed deliberately to the other side of the car. I supposed there'd be a curious crowd around there all day with little boys searching for dark spots in the dust and some garrulous man telling over and over what had

60 happened until it became less and less real even to him and he could tell it no longer and Myrtle Wilson's tragic achievement was forgotten. Now I want to go back a little and tell what happened at the garage after we left there the night before.

---

4 **corroborate sth.**: confirm or give support to sth.   10 **bunch** (infml): group of people   14 **be in cahoots** (AE infml): (here) share an important secret   15 **rag**: any clothes   18 **corruption**: (here) involvement in illegal affairs   19 **incorruptible**: that cannot be destroyed   24 **quotation**: *Börsen-, Kursnotierung*   **interminable**: lasting too long and therefore being boring   30 **divot**: piece of turf cut out by a golf club when making a stroke   31 **golf links**: golf course   33 **Hempstead**: town in Long Island   34 **Southhampton**: town on the south coast of Long Island   52 **central** (old use): telephone operator   59 **garrulous** [ˈgærələs]: talking too much, esp. about unimportant things

They had difficulty in locating the sister, Catherine. She must have broken her rule against drinking that night for when she arrived she was stupid with liquor and unable to understand that the ambulance had already gone to Flushing. When they convinced her of this she immediately fainted as if that was the intolerable part of the affair. Someone 5 kind or curious took her in his car and drove her in the wake of her sister's body.

Until long after midnight a changing crowd lapped up against the front of the garage while George Wilson rocked himself back and forth on the couch inside. For a while the door of the office was open and 10 everyone who came into the garage glanced irresistibly through it. Finally someone said it was a shame and closed the door. Michaelis and several other men were with him—first four or five men, later two or three men. Still later Michaelis had to ask the last stranger to wait there fifteen minutes longer while he went back to his own place and made a 15 pot of coffee. After that he stayed there alone with Wilson until dawn.

About three o'clock the quality of Wilson's incoherent muttering changed—he grew quieter and began to talk about the yellow car. He announced that he had a way of finding out whom the yellow car belonged to, and then he blurted out that a couple of months ago his 20 wife had come from the city with her face bruised and her nose swollen.

But when he heard himself say this he flinched and began to cry "Oh, my God!" again in his groaning voice. Michaelis made a clumsy attempt to distract him. 25

"How long have you been married, George? Come on there, try and sit still a minute and answer my question. How long have you been married?"

"Twelve years."

"Ever had any children? Come on, George, sit still—I asked you a 30 question. Did you ever have any children?"

The hard brown beetles kept thudding against the dull light and whenever Michaelis heard a car go tearing along the road outside it sounded to him like the car that hadn't stopped a few hours before. He didn't like to go into the garage because the work bench was stained 35 where the body had been lying, so he moved uncomfortably around the office—he knew every object in it before morning—and from time to time sat down beside Wilson trying to keep him more quiet.

"Have you got a church you go to sometimes, George? Maybe even if
40 you haven't been there for a long time? Maybe I could call up the church and get a priest to come over and he could talk to you, see?"

"Don't belong to any."

"You ought to have a church, George, for times like this. You must have gone to church once. Didn't you get married in a church? Listen,
45 George, listen to me. Didn't you get married in a church?"

"That was a long time ago."

The effort of answering broke the rhythm of his rocking— for a moment he was silent. Then the same half-knowing, half-bewildered look came back into his faded eyes.

50 "Look in the drawer there," he said, pointing at the desk.

"Which drawer?"

"That drawer—that one."

Michaelis opened the drawer nearest his hand. There was nothing in it but a small expensive dog leash made of leather and braided silver. It
55 was apparently new.

"This?" he inquired, holding it up.

Wilson stared and nodded.

"I found it yesterday afternoon. She tried to tell me about it but I knew it was something funny."

60 "You mean your wife bought it?"

"She had it wrapped in tissue paper on her bureau."

Michaelis didn't see anything odd in that and he gave Wilson a dozen reasons why his wife might have bought the dog leash. But conceivably Wilson had heard some of these same explanations before, from Myrtle,

---

4 **Flushing**: section of Queens borough, New York City   6 **wake**: path left by sth.   8 **lap up**: (here) move backwards and forwards   20 **blurt sth. out**: say sth. suddenly and tactlessly   21 **bruise sb.**: cause an injury to sb. by a blow to the body which causes the skin to become darker   23 **flinch**: move or draw back suddenly, from pain, fear, etc.   25 **distract sb.**: stop sb. concentrating on sth.   32 **beetle**: *Käfer*   **thud against sth.**: hit sth. with a low dull sound   33 **tear along**: (here) move very quickly   54 **braid**: decorate with material woven together in a narrow ornamental band

because he began saying "Oh, my God!" again in a whisper—his comforter left several explanations in the air.

"Then he killed her," said Wilson. His mouth dropped open suddenly.

"Who did?" 5

"I have a way of finding out."

"You're morbid, George," said his friend. "This has been a strain to you and you don't know what you're saying. You'd better try and sit quiet till morning."

"He murdered her." 10

"It was an accident, George."

Wilson shook his head. His eyes narrowed and his mouth widened slightly with the ghost of a superior "Hm!"

"I know," he said definitely. "I'm one of these trusting fellas and I don't think any harm to nobody, but when I get to know a thing I 15 know it. It was the man in that car. She ran out to speak to him and he wouldn't stop."

Michaelis had seen this too but it hadn't occurred to him that there was any special significance in it. He believed that Mrs. Wilson had been running away from her husband, rather than trying to stop any particular 20 car.

"How could she of been like that?"

"She's a deep one," said Wilson, as if that answered the question. "Ah-h-h——"

He began to rock again and Michaelis stood twisting the leash in his 25 hand.

"Maybe you got some friend that I could telephone for, George?"

This was a forlorn hope—he was almost sure that Wilson had no friend: there was not enough of him for his wife. He was glad a little later when he noticed a change in the room, a blue quickening by the 30 window, and realized that dawn wasn't far off. About five o'clock it was blue enough outside to snap off the light.

Wilson's glazed eyes turned out to the ashheaps, where small grey clouds took on fantastic shape and scurried here and there in the faint dawn wind. 35

"I spoke to her," he muttered, after a long silence. "I told her she might fool me but she couldn't fool God. I took her to the window—"

With an effort he got up and walked to the rear window and leaned with his face pressed against it, "—and I said 'God knows what you've been
40 doing, everything you've been doing. You may fool me but you can't fool God!'"

Standing behind him Michaelis saw with a shock that he was looking at the eyes of Doctor T. J. Eckleburg which had just emerged pale and enormous from the dissolving night.

45 "God sees everything," repeated Wilson.

"That's an advertisement," Michaelis assured him. Something made him turn away from the window and look back into the room. But Wilson stood there a long time, his face close to the window pane, nodding into the twilight.

50 By six o'clock Michaelis was worn out and grateful for the sound of a car stopping outside. It was one of the watchers of the night before who had promised to come back so he cooked breakfast for three which he and the other man ate together. Wilson was quieter now and Michaelis went home to sleep; when he awoke four hours later and hurried back
55 to the garage, Wilson was gone.

His movements—he was on foot all the time—were afterward traced to Port Roosevelt and then to Gad's Hill where he bought a sandwich that he didn't eat and a cup of coffee. He must have been tired and walking slowly for he didn't reach Gad's Hill until noon. Thus far there
60 was no difficulty in accounting for his time—there were boys who had seen a man "acting sort of crazy" and motorists at whom he stared oddly from the side of the road. Then for three hours he disappeared from view. The police, on the strength of what he said to Michaelis, that he "had a way of finding out," supposed that he spent that time going from
65 garage to garage thereabouts inquiring for a yellow car. On the other hand no garage man who had seen him ever came forward—and perhaps he had an easier, surer way of finding out what he wanted to know. By

---

2 **comforter**: person who helps sb. who is depressed, etc.   7 **morbid**: having or showing an interest in gloomy or unpleasant matters   28 **forlorn hope**: plan that is almost certain not so succeed   30 **(blue) quickening**: (here) gradual appearance of daylight   34 **scurry**: move quickly   63 **on the strength of sth.**: on the basis of sth.   65 **thereabouts**: somewhere near there   66 **come forward**: present oneself to the police with information

half past two he was in West Egg where he asked someone the way to Gatsby's house. So by that time he knew Gatsby's name.

At two o'clock Gatsby put on his bathing suit and left word with the butler that if anyone phoned word was to be brought to him at the pool. He stopped at the garage for a pneumatic mattress that had amused his 5 guests during the summer, and the chauffeur helped him pump it up. Then he gave instructions that the open car wasn't to be taken out under any circumstances—and this was strange because the front right fender needed repair.

Gatsby shouldered the mattress and started for the pool. Once he 10 stopped and shifted it a little and the chauffeur asked him if he needed help, but he shook his head and in a moment disappeared among the yellowing trees.

No telephone message arrived but the butler went without his sleep and waited for it until four o'clock—until long after there was anyone to 15 give it to if it came. I have an idea that Gatsby himself didn't believe it would come and perhaps he no longer cared. If that was true he must have felt that he had lost the old warm world, paid a high price for living too long with a single dream. He must have looked up at an unfamiliar sky through frightening leaves and shivered as he found what 20 a grotesque thing a rose is and how raw the sunlight was upon the scarcely created grass. A new world, material without being real, where poor ghosts, breathing dreams like air, drifted fortuitously about … like that ashen, fantastic figure gliding toward him through the amorphous trees. 25

The chauffeur—he was one of Wolfshiem's protégés—heard the shots—afterward he could only say that he hadn't thought anything much about them. I drove from the station directly to Gatsby's house and my rushing anxiously up the front steps was the first thing that alarmed anyone. But they knew then, I firmly believe. With scarcely a 30 word said, four of us, the chauffeur, butler, gardener and I, hurried down to the pool.

There was a faint, barely perceptible movement of the water as the fresh flow from one end urged its way toward the drain at the other. With little ripples that were hardly the shadows of waves, the laden 35 mattress moved irregularly down the pool. A small gust of wind that

scarcely corrugated the surface was enough to disturb its accidental course with its accidental burden. The touch of a cluster of leaves revolved it slowly, tracing, like the leg of a compass, a thin red circle in
40   the water.

It was after we started with Gatsby toward the house that the gardener saw Wilson's body a little way off in the grass, and the holocaust was complete.

---

3 **leave word**: give a message   5 **pneumatic mattress** [nuːˈmætɪk] (old use): air mattress   21 **raw**: (here) brutal   23 **fortuitous** [fɔːrˈtuːətəs](fml): happening by chance   24 **amorphous**: having no definite shape   35 **ripple**: small wave or series of waves   **laden** [ˈleɪdən]: bearing the weight of sth.   38 **cluster**: number of things grouped closely together   39 **trace sth.**: draw, outline sth.   **compass**: *Zirkel*   42 **holocaust**: great loss of human life

Chapter 9

After two years I remember the rest of that day, and that night and the next day, only as an endless drill of police and photographers and newspaper men in and out of Gatsby's front door. A rope stretched across the main gate and a policeman by it kept out the curious, but little boys soon discovered that they could enter through my yard and there were always a few of them clustered open-mouthed about the pool. Someone with a positive manner, perhaps a detective, used the expression "mad man" as he bent over Wilson's body that afternoon, and the adventitious authority of his voice set the key for the newspaper reports next morning.

Most of those reports were a nightmare—grotesque, circumstantial, eager and untrue. When Michaelis's testimony at the inquest brought to light Wilson's suspicions of his wife I thought the whole tale would shortly be served up in racy pasquinade—but Catherine, who might have said anything, didn't say a word. She showed a surprising amount of character about it too—looked at the coroner with determined eyes under that corrected brow of hers and swore that her sister had never seen Gatsby, that her sister was completely happy with her husband, that her sister had been into no mischief whatever. She convinced herself of it and cried into her handkerchief as if the very suggestion was more than she could endure. So Wilson was reduced to a man "deranged by grief" in order that the case might remain in its simplest form. And it rested there.

But all this part of it seemed remote and unessential. I found myself on Gatsby's side, and alone. From the moment I telephoned news of the catastrophe to West Egg Village, every surmise about him, and every practical question, was referred to me. At first I was surprised and confused; then as he lay in his house and didn't move or breathe or speak hour upon hour it grew upon me that I was responsible, because no one else was interested—interested, I mean, with that intense personal interest to which everyone has some vague right at the end.

I called up Daisy half an hour after we found him, called her instinctively and without hesitation. But she and Tom had gone away early that afternoon, and taken baggage with them.

35 "Left no address?"

"No."

"Say when they'd be back?"

"No."

"Any idea where they are? How I could reach them?"

40 "I don't know. Can't say."

I wanted to get somebody for him. I wanted to go into the room where he lay and reassure him: "I'll get somebody for you, Gatsby. Don't worry. Just trust me and I'll get somebody for you——"

Meyer Wolfshiem's name wasn't in the phone book. The butler gave 45 me his office address on Broadway and I called Information, but by the time I had the number it was long after five and no one answered the phone.

"Will you ring again?"

"I've rung them three times."

50 "It's very important."

"Sorry. I'm afraid no one's there."

I went back to the drawing room and thought for an instant that they were chance visitors, all these official people who suddenly filled it. But as they drew back the sheet and looked at Gatsby with unmoved eyes, 55 his protest continued in my brain.

"Look here, old sport, you've got to get somebody for me. You've got to try hard. I can't go through this alone."

Someone started to ask me questions but I broke away and going upstairs looked hastily through the unlocked parts of his desk—he'd

---

2 **drill**: (here) repetitive movement   9 **adventitious** (fml): accidental, not necessarily real   12 **testimony**: written or spoken statement declaring that sth. is true   **inquest**: official inquiry to discover facts, esp. about a death which may not have been the result of natural causes   14 **racy** (infml): slightly indecent **pasquinade**: written satire, which is usu. displayed to the public (e.g. in a newspaper or magazine)   16 **coroner**: official who investigates any violent or suspicious death   19 **mischief**: wrong-doing, behavior that causes damage or harm 21 **deranged** (adj): unable to think and act normally   22 **grief**: deep sadness 26 **surmise** [sər'maɪz] (fml): guess   53 **chance** (adj): accidental, unplanned

never told me definitely that his parents were dead. But there was nothing—only the picture of Dan Cody, a token of forgotten violence staring down from the wall.

Next morning I sent the butler to New York with a letter to Wolfshiem which asked for information and urged him to come out on the next train. That request seemed superfluous when I wrote it. I was sure he'd start when he saw the newspapers, just as I was sure there'd be a wire from Daisy before noon—but neither a wire nor Mr. Wolfshiem arrived, no one arrived, except more police and photographers and newspaper men. When the butler brought back Wolfshiem's answer I began to have a feeling of defiance, of scornful solidarity between Gatsby and me against them all.

Dear Mr. Carraway.   This has been one of the most terrible shocks of my life to me I hardly can believe it that it is true at all. Such a mad act as that man did should make us all think, I cannot come down now as I am tied up in some very important business and cannot get mixed up in this thing now. If there is anything I can do a little later let me know in a letter by Edgar. I hardly know where I am when I hear about a thing like this and am completely knocked down and out.

Yours truly

      MEYER WOLFSHIEM

and then hasty addenda beneath:

Let me know about the funeral etc do not know his family at all.

When the phone rang that afternoon and Long Distance said Chicago was calling I thought this would be Daisy at last. But the connection came through as a man's voice, very thin and far away.

"This is Slagle speaking. . . ."

"Yes?" The name was unfamiliar.

"Hell of a note, isn't it? Get my wire?"

"There haven't been any wires."

"Young Parke's in trouble," he said rapidly. "They picked him up when he handed the bonds over the counter. They got a circular from

New York giving 'em the numbers just five minutes before. What d'you know about that, hey? You never can tell in these hick towns——"

35 "Hello!" I interrupted breathlessly. "Look here—this isn't Mr. Gatsby. Mr. Gatsby's dead."

There was a long silence on the other end of the wire followed by an exclamation … then a quick squawk as the connection was broken.

I think it was on the third day that a telegram signed Henry C. Gatz
40 arrived from a town in Minnesota. It said only that the sender was leaving immediately and to postpone the funeral until he came.

It was Gatsby's father, a solemn old man, very helpless and dismayed, bundled up in a long cheap ulster against the warm September day. His eyes leaked continuously with excitement and when I took the bag and
45 umbrella from his hands, he began to pull so incessantly at his sparse grey beard that I had difficulty in getting off his coat. He was on the point of collapse so I took him into the music room and made him sit down while I sent for something to eat. But he wouldn't eat and the glass of milk spilled from his trembling hand.

50 "I saw it in the Chicago newspaper," he said. "It was all in the Chicago newspaper. I started right away."

"I didn't know how to reach you."

His eyes, seeing nothing, moved ceaselessly about the room.

"It was a mad man," he said. "He must have been mad."

55 "Wouldn't you like some coffee?" I urged him.

"I don't want anything. I'm all right now, Mr.——"

"Carraway."

2 **token**: sign, symbol   6 **superfluous**: more than is needed or wanted   7 **wire** (old use): telegram   11 **defiance**: open resistance   **scornful**: showing or feeling strong disrespect   22 **addendum** (pl **addenda**): sth. added; an addition   24 **Long Distance**: long-distance telephone operator   31 **pick sb. up**: seize and arrest sb. 32 **bond**: official paper promising to pay a sum of money to the person who holds it **counter**: *Schalter*   34 **hick** (infml AE, derog): provincial; not sophisticated 38 **squawk**: loud harsh sound   41 **postpone sth.**: arrange sth. to take place at a later time   42 **solemn**: looking very serious   **dismay sb.**: fill sb. with alarm or shock   43 **bundle sb. up**: dress sb. in warm clothes   **ulster**: type of loose, heavy overcoat   45 **incessant**: not stopping, continual   **sparse**: thin, not dense 49 **tremble**: shake involuntarily (from fear, weakness, etc.)   51 **start**: (here) begin a journey   53 **ceaseless**: not stopping, continuous

"Well, I'm all right now. Where have they got Jimmy?"

I took him into the drawing room where his son lay, and left him there. Some little boys had come up on the steps and were looking into the hall; when I told them who had arrived they went reluctantly away.

After a little while Mr. Gatz opened the door and came out, his mouth ajar, his face flushed slightly, his eyes leaking isolated and unpunctual tears. He had reached an age where death no longer has the quality of ghastly surprise, and when he looked around him now for the first time and saw the height and splendor of the hall and the great rooms opening out from it into other rooms, his grief began to be mixed with an awed pride. I helped him to a bedroom upstairs; while he took off his coat and vest I told him that all arrangements had been deferred until he came.

"I didn't know what you'd want, Mr. Gatsby——"

"Gatz is my name."

"——Mr. Gatz. I thought you might want to take the body West."

He shook his head.

"Jimmy always liked it better down East. He rose up to his position in the East. Were you a friend of my boy's, Mr.——?"

"We were close friends."

"He had a big future before him, you know. He was only a young man, but he had a lot of brain power here."

He touched his head impressively and I nodded.

"If he'd of lived he'd of been a great man. A man like James J. Hill. He'd of helped build up the country."

"That's true," I said uncomfortably.

He fumbled at the embroidered coverlet, trying to take it from the bed, and lay down stiffly—was instantly asleep.

That night an obviously frightened person called up and demanded to know who I was before he would give his name.

"This is Mr. Carraway," I said.

"Oh—" He sounded relieved. "This is Klipspringer."

I was relieved too, for that seemed to promise another friend at Gatsby's grave. I didn't want it to be in the papers and draw a sightseeing crowd, so I'd been calling up a few people myself. They were hard to find.

"The funeral's tomorrow," I said. "Three o'clock here at the house. I wish you'd tell anybody who'd be interested."

"Oh, I will," he broke out hastily. "Of course I'm not likely to see anybody, but if I do."

40   His tone made me suspicious.

"Of course you'll be there yourself."

"Well, I'll certainly try. What I called up about is——"

"Wait a minute," I interrupted. "How about saying you'll come?"

"Well, the fact is—the truth of the matter is that I'm staying with

45   some people up here in Greenwich and they rather expect me to be with them tomorrow. In fact there's a sort of picnic or something. Of course I'll do my very best to get away."

I ejaculated an unrestrained "Huh!" and he must have heard me for he went on nervously:

50   "What I called up about was a pair of shoes I left there. I wonder if it'd be too much trouble to have the butler send them on. You see they're tennis shoes and I'm sort of helpless without them. My address is care of B. F.——"

I didn't hear the rest of the name because I hung up the receiver.

55   After that I felt a certain shame for Gatsby—one gentleman to whom I telephoned implied that he had got what he deserved. However, that was my fault, for he was one of those who used to sneer most bitterly at Gatsby on the courage of Gatsby's liquor and I should have known better than to call him.

60   The morning of the funeral I went up to New York to see Meyer Wolfshiem; I couldn't seem to reach him any other way. The door that I pushed open on the advice of an elevator boy was marked "The Swastika Holding Company" and at first there didn't seem to be anyone inside. But when I'd shouted "Hello" several times in vain, an argument broke

65   out behind a partition, and presently a lovely Jewess appeared at an interior door and scrutinized me with black hostile eyes.

---

6 **flush** (v): (of a face) become red   **unpunctual**: (here) coming at different times
23 **James J. Hill** (1838–1916): US railroad magnate and financier, who lived in
St. Paul's, Minnesota   26 **embroider sth.**: decorate sth. with needlework
45 **Greenwich** ['grenɪtʃ]: wealthy town in Connecticut   48 **ejaculate** (fml): exclaim
unrestrained: not controlled   57 **sneer at sb./sth.**: express contempt for sb./sth.
62 **swastika**: mystic symbol in various cultures; *Hakenkreuz*   65 **partition**:
structure that divides a room into two parts

"Nobody's in," she said. "Mr. Wolfshiem's gone to Chicago."

The first part of this was obviously untrue for someone had begun to whistle "The Rosary," tunelessly, inside.

"Please say that Mr. Carraway wants to see him."

"I can't get him back from Chicago, can I?"   5

At this moment a voice unmistakably Wolfshiem's called "Stella!" from the other side of the door.

"Leave your name on the desk," she said quickly. "I'll give it to him when he gets back."

"But I know he's there."   10

She took a step toward me and began to slide her hands indignantly up and down her hips.

"You young men think you can force your way in here any time," she scolded. "We're getting sickantired of it. When I say he's in Chicago he's in Chicago."   15

I mentioned Gatsby.

"Oh-h!" She looked at me over again. "Will you just——what was your name?"

She vanished. In a moment Meyer Wolfshiem stood solemnly in the doorway, holding out both hands. He drew me into his office, remarking   20 in a reverent voice that it was a sad time for all of us, and offered me a cigar.

"My memory goes back to when first I met him," he said. "A young major just out of the army and covered over with medals he got in the war. He was so hard up he had to keep on wearing his uniform because   25 he couldn't buy some regular clothes. First time I saw him was when he come into Winebrenner's poolroom at Forty-Third Street and asked for a job. He hadn't eat anything for a couple of days. 'Come on have some lunch with me,' I sid. He ate more than four dollars' worth of food in half an hour."   30

"Did you start him in business?" I inquired.

"Start him! I made him."

"Oh."

"I raised him up out of nothing, right out of the gutter. I saw right away he was a fine-appearing gentlemanly young man and when he told   35 me he was an Oggsford I knew I could use him good. I got him to join up in the American Legion and he used to stand high there. Right off he did some work for a client of mine up to Albany. We were so thick like that in everything—" He held up two bulbous fingers "—always

40 together."

I wondered if this partnership had included the World's Series transaction in 1919.

"Now he's dead," I said after a moment. "You were his closest friend, so I know you'll want to come to his funeral this afternoon."

45 "I'd like to come."

"Well, come then."

The hair in his nostrils quivered slightly and as he shook his head his eyes filled with tears.

"I can't do it—I can't get mixed up in it," he said.

50 "There's nothing to get mixed up in. It's all over now."

"When a man gets killed I never like to get mixed up in it in any way. I keep out. When I was a young man it was different—if a friend of mine died, no matter how, I stuck with them to the end. You may think that's sentimental but I mean it—to the bitter end."

55 I saw that for some reason of his own he was determined not to come, so I stood up.

"Are you a college man?" he inquired suddenly.

For a moment I thought he was going to suggest a "gonnegtion" but he only nodded and shook my hand.

60 "Let us learn to show our friendship for a man when he is alive and not after he is dead," he suggested. "After that my own rule is to let everything alone."

When I left his office the sky had turned dark and I got back to West Egg in a drizzle. After changing my clothes I went next door and found

65 Mr. Gatz walking up and down excitedly in the hall. His pride in his son and in his son's possessions was continually increasing and now he had something to show me.

"Jimmy sent me this picture." He took out his wallet with trembling fingers. "Look there."

3 **"The Rosary"**: song by Ethelbert Nevin and R.C. Rogers, published in 1898 but popular in the 1920s   14 **sickantired** (non-standard pron): sick and tired
21 **reverent**: feeling or showing great respect   25 **be hard up**: be short of money
34 **the gutter** (sl): poor state of life   38 **Albany**: capital of New York State
39 **bulbous**: round and fat   64 **drizzle**: light rain

It was a photograph of the house, cracked in the corners and dirty with many hands. He pointed out every detail to me eagerly. "Look there!" and then sought admiration from my eyes. He had shown it so often that I think it was more real to him now than the house itself.

"Jimmy sent it to me. I think it's a very pretty picture. It shows up   5 well."

"Very well. Had you seen him lately?"

"He come out to see me two years ago and bought me the house I live in now. Of course we was broke up when he run off from home but I see now there was a reason for it. He knew he had a big future in front   10 of him. And ever since he made a success he was very generous with me."

He seemed reluctant to put away the picture, held it for another minute, lingeringly, before my eyes. Then he returned the wallet and pulled from his pocket a ragged old copy of a book called   15 "Hopalong Cassidy."

"Look here, this is a book he had when he was a boy. It just shows you."

He opened it at the back cover and turned it around for me to see. On the last fly-leaf was printed the word SCHEDULE, and the date   20 September 12th, 1906. And underneath:

Rise from bed	6.00	A.M.	
Dumbbell exercise and wall-scaling	6.15–6.30	"	
Study electricity, etc.	7.15–8.15	"	
Work	8.30–4.30	P.M.	25
Baseball and sports	4.30–5.00	"	
Practice elocution, poise and how to			
attain it	5.00–6.00	"	
Study needed inventions	7.00–9.00	"	

GENERAL RESOLVES   30

No wasting time at Shafters or [a name, indecipherable]
No more smoking or chewing
Bath every other day
Read one improving book or magazine per week

35   Save $ 5.00 [crossed out] $ 3.00 per week
Be better to parents

"I come across this book by accident," said the old man. "It just shows you, don't it?"

"It just shows you."

40   "Jimmy was bound to get ahead. He always had some resolves like this or something. Do you notice what he's got about improving his mind? He was always great for that. He told me I et like a hog once and I beat him for it."

He was reluctant to close the book, reading each item aloud and then 45 looking eagerly at me. I think he rather expected me to copy down the list for my own use.

A little before three the Lutheran minister arrived from Flushing, and I began to look involuntarily out the windows for other cars. So did Gatsby's father. And as the time passed and the servants came in and 50 stood waiting in the hall, his eyes began to blink anxiously and he spoke of the rain in a worried, uncertain way. The minister glanced several times at his watch so I took him aside and asked him to wait for half an hour. But it wasn't any use. Nobody came.

About five o'clock our procession of three cars reached the cemetery 55 and stopped in a thick drizzle beside the gate—first a motor hearse, horribly black and wet, then Mr. Gatz and the minister and I in the limousine, and, a little later, four or five servants and the postman from West Egg in Gatsby's station wagon, all wet to the skin. As we started through the gate into the cemetery I heard a car stop and then the sound 60 of someone splashing after us over the soggy ground. I looked around.

---

14 **lingering**: remaining   16 "**Hopalong Cassidy**": cowboy book by Clarence E. Mulford, first published in 1910   20 **fly-leaf**: blank page at the beginning or end of a book   23 **dumbbell**: *Hantel*   **wall-scaling**: *Sprossenwand klettern* 27 **elocution**: art of speaking clearly and effectively, esp. in public   **poise**: graceful and balanced (control of) bodily position or movement   30 **resolve** (fml): sth. one has decided to do   31 **indecipherable**: *unentzifferbar*   40 **bound to do sth.**: certain to do sth.   42 **et** (non-standard pron): ate   **hog**: pig reared for meat 44 **reluctant**: unwilling   55 **hearse**: *Leichenwagen*   58 **station wagon** (AE): *Kombiwagen*   60 **soggy**: very wet; heavy with water

It was the man with owl-eyed glasses whom I had found marvelling over
Gatsby's books in the library one night three months before.

I'd never seen him since then. I don't know how he knew about the
funeral or even his name. The rain poured down his thick glasses and he
took them off and wiped them to see the protecting canvas unrolled   5
from Gatsby's grave.

I tried to think about Gatsby then for a moment, but he was already
too far away and I could only remember, without resentment, that Daisy
hadn't sent a message or a flower. Dimly I heard someone murmur
"Blessed are the dead that the rain falls on," and then the owl-eyed man   10
said "Amen to that," in a brave voice.

We straggled down quickly through the rain to the cars. Owl Eyes
spoke to me by the gate.

"I couldn't get to the house," he remarked.

"Neither could anybody else."   15

"Go on!" He started. "Why, my God! They used to go there by the
hundreds."

He took off his glasses and wiped them again outside and in.

"The poor son-of-a-bitch," he said.

One of my most vivid memories is of coming back west from prep   20
school and later from college at Christmas time. Those who went farther
than Chicago would gather in the old dim Union Station at six o'clock of
a December evening with a few Chicago friends already caught up into
their own holiday gayeties to bid them a hasty goodbye. I remember the
fur coats of the girls returning from Miss This or That's and the chatter   25
of frozen breath and the hands waving overhead as we caught sight of
old acquaintances and the matchings of invitations: "Are you going to
the Ordways'? the Herseys'? the Schultzes'?" and the long green tickets
clasped tight in our gloved hands. And last the murky yellow cars of the
Chicago, Milwaukee & St. Paul Railroad looking cheerful as Christmas   30
itself on the tracks beside the gate.

When we pulled out into the winter night and the real snow, our
snow, began to stretch out beside us and twinkle against the windows,
and the dim lights of small Wisconsin stations moved by, a sharp wild
brace came suddenly into the air. We drew in deep breaths of it as we   35
walked back from dinner through the cold vestibules, unutterably aware

of our identity with this country for one strange hour before we melted indistinguishably into it again.

That's my middle-west—not the wheat or the prairies or the lost
40   Swede towns, but the thrilling, returning trains of my youth and the street lamps and sleigh bells in the frosty dark and the shadows of holly wreaths thrown by lighted windows on the snow. I am part of that, a little solemn with the feel of those long winters, a little complacent from growing up in the Carraway house in a city where dwellings are still
45   called through decades by a family's name. I see now that this has been a story of the West, after all—Tom and Gatsby, Daisy and Jordan and I, were all Westerners, and perhaps we possessed some deficiency in common which made us subtly unadaptable to Eastern life.

Even when the East excited me most, even when I was most keenly
50   aware of its superiority to the bored, sprawling, swollen towns beyond the Ohio, with their interminable inquisitions which spared only the children and the very old—even then it had always for me a quality of distortion. West Egg especially still figures in my more fantastic dreams. I see it as a night scene by El Greco: a hundred houses, at once conven-
55   tional and grotesque, crouching under a sullen, overhanging sky and a lustreless moon. In the foreground four solemn men in dress suits are walking along the sidewalk with a stretcher on which lies a drunken

1 **marvel over** (usu. **at**) **sth.** (fml): be filled with wonder, surprise and admiration at sth.   8 **resentment**: bitterness or anger   12 **straggle**: walk in scattered, irregular order   16 **Go on!**: I don't believe it!   19 **son of a bitch** (sl): (here) fellow, man 20–21 **prep school = preparatory school**: (in the USA) private secondary school preparing students for college   24 **gayeties**: festivities   **bid sb. sth.**: say sth. (e.g. a greeting or goodbye) to sb.   25 **Miss This or That's**: many private girls' schools have names that begin with "Miss"   **chatter**: continuous rapid talk   27 **matching** (n): (here) comparison   29 **clasp sb./sth.**: hold sb./sth. tightly   **murky**: dark, dirty 35 **brace**: (here) feeling or smell of freshness   36 **unutterable**: that cannot be said or put into words   41 **sleigh** [sleɪ]: *Pferdeschlitten*   41–42 **holly wreath**: *Kranz aus Stechpalmenzweigen*   43 **complacent** [kəmˈpleɪsənt]: generally satisfied with oneself   48 **subtle** [ˈsʌtəl]: not easy to detect or describe   **unadaptable**: anpassungsunfähig   50 **sprawl**: spread out loosely and irregularly over much space **swell – swelled – swollen**: become larger   51 **Ohio = Ohio River**: river in the eastern USA   **inquisition** (fml): questioning about one's private affairs   54 **El Greco = Domenikos Theotocopoulos** (1541–1614): Spanish painter of Greek origin   56 **lustreless** [ˈlʌstərləs]: without brightness or shine   57 **stretcher**: covered frame on which a sick person can be carried by two people

woman in a white evening dress. Her hand, which dangles over the side, sparkles cold with jewels. Gravely the men turn in at a house—the wrong house. But no one knows the woman's name, and no one cares.

After Gatsby's death the East was haunted for me like that, distorted beyond my eyes' power of correction. So when the blue smoke of brittle 5 leaves was in the air and the wind blew the wet laundry stiff on the line I decided to come back home.

There was one thing to be done before I left, an awkward, unpleasant thing that perhaps had better have been let alone. But I wanted to leave things in order and not just trust that obliging and indifferent sea to 10 sweep my refuse away. I saw Jordan Baker and talked over and around what had happened to us together and what had happened afterward to me, and she lay perfectly still, listening, in a big chair.

She was dressed to play golf and I remember thinking she looked like a good illustration, her chin raised a little, jauntily, her hair the color 15 of an autumn leaf, her face the same brown tint as the fingerless glove on her knee. When I had finished she told me without comment that she was engaged to another man. I doubted that though there were several she could have married at a nod of her head, but I pretended to be surprised. For just a minute I wondered if I wasn't making a mistake, 20 then I thought it all over again quickly and got up to say goodbye.

"Nevertheless you did throw me over," said Jordan suddenly. "You threw me over on the telephone. I don't give a damn about you now but it was a new experience for me and I felt a little dizzy for a while."

We shook hands. 25

"Oh, and do you remember—" she added, "—a conversation we had once about driving a car?"

"Why,—not exactly."

"You said a bad driver was only safe until she met another bad driver? Well, I met another bad driver, didn't I? I mean it was careless of me to 30 make such a wrong guess. I thought you were rather an honest, straightforward person. I thought it was your secret pride."

"I'm thirty," I said. "I'm five years too old to lie to myself and call it honor."

She didn't answer. Angry, and half in love with her, and tremendously 35 sorry, I turned away.

One afternoon late in October I saw Tom Buchanan. He was walking ahead of me along Fifth Avenue in his alert, aggressive way, his hands out a little from his body as if to fight off interference, his head moving
40 sharply here and there, adapting itself to his restless eyes. Just as I slowed up to avoid overtaking him he stopped and began frowning into the windows of a jewelry store. Suddenly he saw me and walked back holding out his hand.

"What's the matter, Nick? Do you object to shaking hands with me?"
45 "Yes. You know what I think of you."

"You're crazy, Nick," he said quickly. "Crazy as hell. I don't know what's the matter with you."

"Tom," I inquired, "what did you say to Wilson that afternoon?"

He stared at me without a word and I knew I had guessed right about
50 those missing hours. I started to turn away but he took a step after me and grabbed my arm.

"I told him the truth," he said. "He came to the door while we were getting ready to leave and when I sent down word that we weren't in he tried to force his way upstairs. He was crazy enough to kill me if I hadn't
55 told him who owned the car. His hand was on a revolver in his pocket every minute he was in the house——" He broke off defiantly. "What if I did tell him? That fellow had it coming to him. He threw dust into your eyes just like he did in Daisy's, but he was a tough one. He ran over Myrtle like you'd run over a dog and never even stopped his car."

60 There was nothing I could say, except the one unutterable fact that it wasn't true.

"And if you think I didn't have my share of suffering—look here, when I went to give up that flat and saw that damn box of dog biscuits sitting there on the sideboard I sat down and cried like a baby. By God it
65 was awful——"

---

1 **dangle**: hang or wing loosely   2 **grave** (adj): very serious in manner
4 **haunt sb.**: (esp. of sth. strange or sad) be always in the thoughts of sb.   5 **brittle**:
(here) dried up   11 **refuse** (n): rubbish   19 **at a nod of her head**: whenever she
wished   22 **throw sb. over** (old-fashioned, infml): surprise sb.   24 **dizzy**: confused
34 **honor**: strong sense of what is morally right   38 **alert**: attentive and quick to
think or act   41 **frown**: (here) look disapprovingly   57 **have sth. coming to you**:
deserve sth.   57–58 **throw dust into sb.'s eyes**: deceive sb.

I couldn't forgive him or like him but I saw that what he had done was, to him, entirely justified. It was all very careless and confused. They were careless people, Tom and Daisy—they smashed up things and creatures and then retreated back into their money or their vast carelessness or whatever it was that kept them together, and let other people clean up the mess they had made. . . .   5

I shook hands with him; it seemed silly not to, for I felt suddenly as though I were talking to a child. Then he went into the jewelry store to buy a pearl necklace—or perhaps only a pair of cuff buttons—rid of my provincial squeamishness forever.   10

Gatsby's house was still empty when I left—the grass on his lawn had grown as long as mine. One of the taxi drivers in the village never took a fare past the entrance gate without stopping for a minute and pointing inside; perhaps it was he who drove Daisy and Gatsby over to East Egg the night of the accident and perhaps he had made a story about it all   15 his own. I didn't want to hear it and I avoided him when I got off the train.

I spent my Saturday nights in New York because those gleaming, dazzling parties of his were with me so vividly that I could still hear the music and the laughter faint and incessant from his garden and the cars   20 going up and down his drive. One night I did hear a material car there and saw its lights stop at his front steps. But I didn't investigate. Probably it was some final guest who had been away at the ends of the earth and didn't know that the party was over.

On the last night, with my trunk packed and my car sold to the   25 grocer, I went over and looked at that huge incoherent failure of a house once more. On the white steps an obscene word, scrawled by some boy with a piece of brick, stood out clearly in the moonlight and I erased it, drawing my shoe raspingly along the stone. Then I wandered down to the beach and sprawled out on the sand.   30

Most of the big shore places were closed now and there were hardly any lights except the shadowy, moving glow of a ferryboat across the Sound. And as the moon rose higher the inessential houses began to melt away until gradually I became aware of the old island here that flowered once for Dutch sailors' eyes—a fresh, green breast of the new   35 world. Its vanished trees, the trees that had made way for Gatsby's house,

had once pandered in whispers to the last and greatest of all human dreams; for a transitory, enchanted moment man must have held his breath in the presence of this continent, compelled into an æsthetic
40 contemplation he neither understood nor desired, face to face for the last time in history with something commensurate to his capacity for wonder.

And as I sat there, brooding on the old unknown world, I thought of Gatsby's wonder when he first picked out the green light at the end of
45 Daisy's dock. He had come a long way to this blue lawn and his dream must have seemed so close that he could hardly fail to grasp it. He did not know that it was already behind him, somewhere back in that vast obscurity beyond the city, where the dark fields of the republic rolled on under the night.

50 Gatsby believed in the green light, the orgastic future that year by year recedes before us. It eluded us then, but that's no matter—tomorrow we will run faster, stretch out our arms farther. . . . And one fine morning——

So we beat on, boats against the current, borne back ceaselessly into
55 the past.

---

4 **retreat**: *sich zurückziehen*   9 **cuff button**: *Manschettenknopf*   **be rid of sth.**: be free of sth.   10 **squeamishness**: state of being too careful about principles, morals, etc.   13 **fare** (infml): passenger, customer   20 **faint**: not intense in sound **incessant**: not stopping, continual   25 **trunk**: *Schrankkoffer*   26 **incoherent**: not understandable   28 **erase sth.**: remove sth. by rubbing or scraping   29 **rasp**: move roughly, making an unpleasant grating sound   30 **sprawl out**: sit or lie with one's arms and legs spread out loosely   33 **inessential**: insignificant   37 **pander to sb./ sth.** (derog): try to satisfy sb./sth.   38 **transitory**: lasting for only a short time **enchant sb.**: fill sb. with great delight   39 **compel sb.** (fml): force sb. 40 **contemplation**: act of looking at sb./sth. thoughtfully   41 **commensurate to sth.** (fml): in the right proportion to sth.   43 **brood on sth.**: think about sth. for a long time in a sad or troubled way   44 **pick sth. out** (infml): find sth. one is looking for   50 **orgastic**: full of intense excitement and pleasure   51 **recede**: move away from an observer   **elude sb./sth.**: escape or avoid sb./sth.   54 **beat**: (here) move forward despite great resistance   **bear sth. – bore – borne** (fml): carry sth. from one place to another

Map of New York and Long Island

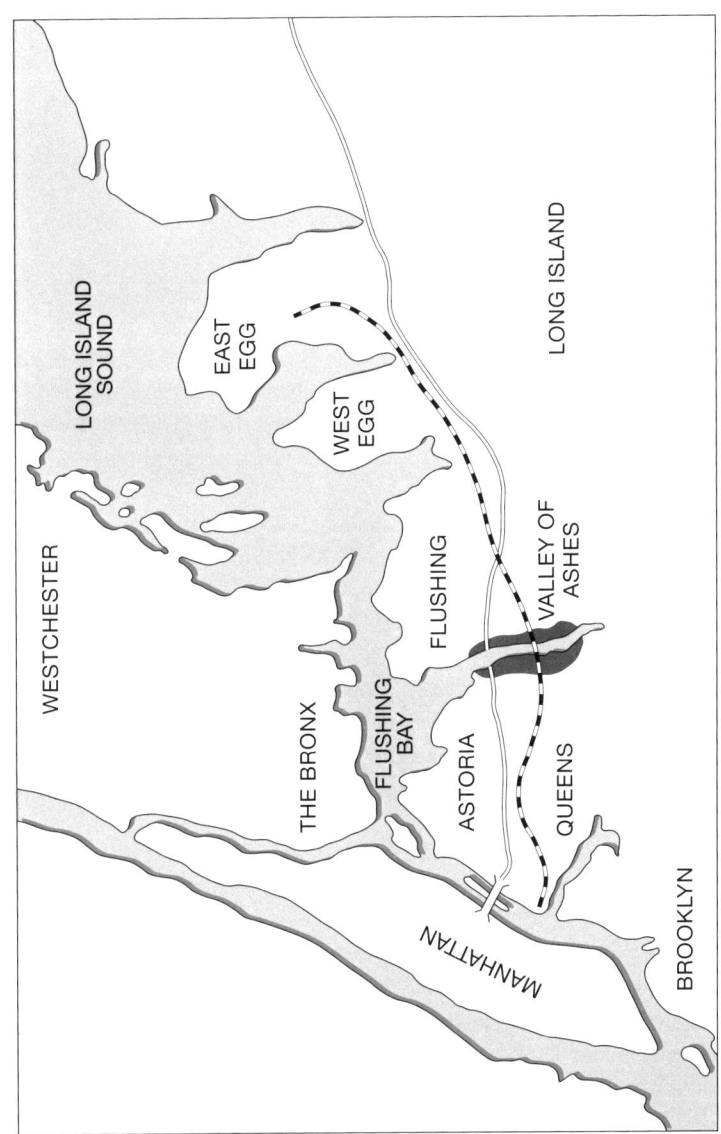

Information about the Author

© mauritius images / Pictorial Press, Pictorial Press Ltd / Alamy / Alamy Stock Photos

Francis Scott Fitzgerald was born in St. Paul, Minnesota in 1896 to an upper-middle-class Catholic family. He attended Princeton University but dropped out before graduating. He joined the army in 1917 when the USA entered the First World War. While a soldier he met Zelda Sayre, who he married in 1920.

His first novel, *This Side of Paradise* (1920) was an instant success. The novel is about a young college man and mirrors much of Fitzgerald's youthful experiences at university. With his success, his glamorous social life, his good looks and intelligence, Fitzgerald came to exemplify the "Jazz Age".

It was his short stories that financed his lifestyle, as his later novels, e.g. *The Beautiful and the Damned* (1922) and *Tender Is the Night* (1934) did not sell too well. His second collection of short stories, *Tales of the Jazz Age* (1922), contained his most famous short story "The Diamond as Big as the Ritz".

His most famous novel *The Great Gatsby* was published in 1925, but it was only after his death that it was fully appreciated.

Fitzgerald and his wife lived for many years in France, where they were friends with Ernest Hemingway and Gertrude Stein. In 1931 the Fitzgeralds moved permanently back to the USA, as Zelda started to suffer from mental instability. At the same time, Fitzgerald had financial problems and started to drink. He went to Hollywood to work as a scriptwriter, but had no success there. He died of a heart attack in 1940.